GREEK LEGENDS
and Stories

M.V. SETON WILLIAMS

The Rubicon Press

The Rubicon Press
57 Cornwall Gardens
London SW7 4BE

A catalogue record for this book is available from the British Library.

ISBN 0 948695 22 6

Printed and bound in Great Britain by Biddles Limited of Guildford and King's Lynn

Contents

I	Introduction	1
II	The Beginning of the World	6
III	The Olympians	9
IV	The Coming of Man	13
V	Hermes	17
VI	Demeter and Persephone	20
VII	The Birth of Apollo and Artemis	23
VIII	The Story of Io	30
IX	Heracles	33
X	The Argonauts and the Search for the Golden Fleece	42
XI	Orpheus and Eurydice	47
XII	The Contest of Poseidon and Athene	50
XIII	Theseus of Attica	52
XIV	Meleager of Calydon	56
XV	Atlanta's Race	59
XVI	Arachne's Web	62
XVII	The Story of Perseus	64
XVIII	Eros and Psyche	66
XIX	Bellerophon and Pegasus the Winged Horse	71
XX	The Faithless King of Troy	73
XXI	The Halcyon Days	75
XXII	Daedalus and the First Flight	77
XXIII	Echo and Narcissus	79
XXIV	Pygmalion and Galatea	81
XXV	Philemon and Baucis	83
XXVI	The House of Cadmus	85
XXVII	Ino Daughter of Cadmus	87
XXVIII	Dionysus	89
XXIX	Artemis and Actaeon	93
XXX	The Story of Oedipus	94
XXXI	The Seven against Thebes	97
XXXII	The Revenge of Alcmaeon	101
XXXIII	The Trojan War	103
XXXIV	Aeneas	112
XXXV	Orestes	114
XXXVI	The Odyssey	117

XXXVII	The Story of Tereus, Procne and Philomela	123
XXXVIII	Phaethon	125
XXXIX	Midas, King of Phrygia	128
XL	The Foundation of Marseilles	130
XLI	Croesus, King of Lydia	133
XLII	Polycrates of Samos	136
XLIII	The Wild Man and the Prince	139
XLIV	The Nereid	145
XLV	The Queen of the Gorgons	150
XLVI	The Three Citrons	154
XLVII	The Tower of the Forty Dhrakos	160
XLVIII	The Strangler Princess	166
XLIX	The Chapel of Ayios Hilarios	169
	Glossary	171
	Bibliography	172
	Index	173

List of Illustrations

1	Zeus fighting the monster Typhon *(Copyright British Museum)*	8
2	Zeus, father of the gods *(Copyright British Museum)*	10
3	The abduction of Europa *(Copyright British Museum)*	16
4	Hermes, the messenger of the gods *(Copyright British Museum)*	18
5	Apollo and Artemis with their mother Leto *(Copyright British Museum)*	23
6	Apollo and Artemis slaying the children of Niobe *(Copyright British Museum)*	29
7	Heracles bringing the boar to Eurystheus *(Copyright British Museum)*	36
8	The building of the *Argo (Copyright British Museum)*	43
9	Orpheus looking back at Eurydice when she returns from the Underworld *(C.M. Dixon)*	48
10	Athene *(Copyright British Museum)*	51
11	Theseus lifting rock to take his father's sword *(C.M. Dixon)*	53
12	Aphrodite, goddess of love*(Copyright British Museum)*	60
13	The winged horse Pegasus *(Copyright British Museum)*	72
14	Dionysus *(Copyright British Museum)*	91
15	Oedipus and the Sphinx *(C.M. Dixon)*	95
16	The judgement of Paris *(Copyright British Museum)*	104
17	Achilles and Ajax playing a board game *(Copyright British Museum)*	108
18	Funeral games in honour of Patroclus *(Copyright British Museum)*	109
19	Odysseus gouging out the single eye of Polyphemus, the Cyclops *(Copyright British Museum)*	119
20	Odysseus and the Sirens *(Copyright British Museum)*	121
21	A Nereid *(Copyright British Museum)*	148
22	The Gorgon *(Copyright British Museum)*	151

For Emma and Alexander
to introduce them to the
stories of Greece, as I was
by E.M. Robb

Acknowledgements

As a child, E.M. Robb gave Veronica Seton-Williams *Greek Wonder Tales* by Lucy M.J. Garnett, a collection of Greek folk tales, which were the start of her lifelong fascination with the legends of many lands. Sadly, Veronica Seton-Williams died just after she had written this book. She had decided to dedicate it to my grandchildren, Emma and Alexander, so that they too could read the stories that enthralled her so much. She also wanted to inspire those who are no longer familiar with the classics and bring enjoyment to others who might like to read them again.

I particularly wish to thank Dr. Susan Walker of the Greek and Roman Antiquities Department at the British Museum for all her help in selecting illustrations and to Anthea Page and Juanita Homan of The Rubicon Press for their encouragement and assistance with the editing, proof reading and indexing.

Angela Godfrey
St. John, Jersey C.I.
1993

Map of Ancient Greece

I

Introduction

The Greek heroic legends form cycles connected with different parts of Greece. Most of them are connected with Minoan/Mycenaean sites and heroes. The original Argonauts are Minyans (Minyai) from the site of Mycenaean Orchomenus. The Theban saga is an account of the struggles of two Mycenaean cities, Thebes and Argos, fighting for supremacy. Heracles, though frequently absent, is connected with Tiryns. Troy is attacked by four Mycenaean cities, Argos, Asine, Mycenae and Sparta. The legend of Theseus is set in Mycenaean Athens and the remains of a Mycenaean palace and fort have been found on the Acropolis.

The Cretan legends of Minos and the Minotaur refer to a pre-Greek age, when Crete held the supremacy of the sea and dominated the mainland cities, exacting tribute; a position later reversed with the rise of the Mycenaean/Achaean states in the Peloponnese, dominated by Mycenae. Although the later Greeks regarded Minos as an early king of Crete, we do not know if this was actually his name, or merely a title like pharaoh or king.

The civilization of the Late Bronze Age in Greece has been called the 'Mycenaean' because it was first discovered by Heinrich Schliemann at Mycenae in 1876. Prior to this, Greek history was thought to have begun in 776 B.C. with the First Olympiad. Mycenae, meaning 'rich in gold', was, at the time of the Trojan War (c. 1200 B.C.), the leading city in the Achaean League but this position was not static and changed frequently. The world of this period is vividly portrayed by Homer, an epic Greek poet, who lived some four hundred years after the events that he described but whose veracity has been attested to, by excavations carried out at Troy, Mycenae, Pylus and other Mycenaean sites. For instance, the boar's tusk helmets which he described and

1

which no one quite believed in, turned up at Cnossus (Knossos) in Crete and there is one from the Peloponnese, now in the Nauplia Museum.

The Mycenaean settlements have certain features in common. The large palaces were always built on fortified acropoli, of a megaron type structure, which later developed into the prototype of the classical temple. The acropolis walls were usually built of large stone blocks known to the later Greeks as Cyclopean because they thought that these vast blocks must have been moved by giants, the Cyclops. The walls of the palaces were decorated with brightly coloured frescos, probably copied from those of Minoan cities, although the palaces themselves were less ornate and much smaller than the Minoan palaces.

The people who founded the Mycenaean civilization were early Greeks, one of several waves of invasions that came into the country through northern Greece from the Balkans. It is known that they were Greek from their writing on the Linear B tablets found on many of the Mycenaean sites, such as Mycenae and Pylus. This script was written on clay tablets and found in the palaces and houses of the period. The writing usually consists of lists of weapons, chariots, stores or goods, although there are references to several deities who occur later in the Classical Period. It is interesting to note that Zeus and Hera are already paired together. Poseidon, Hermes, Athene, Artemis and Apollo make an appearance and there is the goddess Potnia 'the mistress', equated with Demeter, the Corn Goddess. In the texts the gods are only mentioned as the recipients of offerings. For instance, on one tablet, Poseidon received a bull, four rams (the animals were presumably listed for sacrifice), wheat, wine, cheese, honey, perfumes and animal skins.

Mycenaean palaces have been found on the following sites: Mycenae, Tiryns, Pylus, Asine, Iolcus in Thessaly, Athens and Eleusis where the cult of the goddess Demeter dates to this period. Corinth has a palace, though it is not an important site; Argos is identified as the Mycenaean Prosymna, with its Heraion, the great sanctuary to Hera, which is of Mycenaean origin. Mycenaean chamber tombs have also been found in the vicinity. Although no palace has been found at Sparta, extensive Mycenaean remains have been found in the neighbourhood. At Amykli, at the foot of Mount Taygetus, at Stephania, Molaoi, Skala, Neopolis and Boion, extensive Mycenaean remains suggest more settlements. Monovasia's early name of Minoa, suggests that originally it was a Minoan settlement, pre-dating the Mycenaeans.

One of the most important palaces to be excavated was that of Pylus, by the American School of Classical Studies under Carl Blegen. Thought to have been the palace of Nestor, one of the heroes of the Trojan War, it was discovered on the hill of Ano Englianos, eighteen kilometres north of the modern town of Pylus. The site yielded hundreds of tablets inscribed in Linear B. The palace was a two-storied building with a throne room, a circular hearth and the remains of a stairway leading to a second floor, where the sleeping apartments would have been. The main Mycenaean settlement lay below the palace on the slopes of the hill and in addition to domestic buildings there were many *tholoi* and chamber tombs.

Thebes seems to have been an important centre in early Mycenaean times, although its importance appears to have diminished by the time of the Trojan War. There was a Mycenaean palace in the citadel and the remains of workshops producing signet rings, cylinder seals and gem stones of precious and semi-precious stone, often engraved. The Theban Museum contains many painted clay Mycenaean sarcophagi and other objects from the Cadmeion, the citadel which was the centre of Mycenaean power in the city.

The acropolis of Gla, not far from Thebes, is Mycenaean in origin and has both a palace and a possible agora. The acropolis, which is strongly walled, has several imposing Mycenaean gateways. The city of Aulis had an acropolis dating back to Mycenaean times, although the earlier city was situated nearer the coast than the Classical one. Volos, ancient Iolcus, the city reigned over by Peleus, was where Jason set off from, to find the Golden Fleece. The Mycenaean palace is situated on a hill called Palia. On the shore at Nelia, some Mycenaean remains have been discovered, thought to have been ancient shipyards, where the *Argo* was probably built.

On the island of Euboea, off the Boeotian coast, a Mycenaean settlement has been found by the British School in Athens, at the village of Lefkandi near Chalcis, the modern capital of the island. The island of Skyros has many links with Greece's legendary past. It is here Theseus was supposed to have been buried and Achilles was hidden by his mother, Thetis, in an attempt to prevent him going to the Trojan War. It is known that the island was settled at that period, as Mycenaean pottery and tombs have been found there.

The sanctuary of Artemis at Calydon is probably early, although no Mycenaean remains have yet been found but not very much archaeological work has been done in the area. Cythera, one of the Ionian islands off the Peloponnese, had Minoan settlements dating to both the Middle and Late Periods, thus pre-dating the Mycenaean settlements. According to a late tradition, the goddess Aphrodite was born here and not in Cyprus. At Lemnos in the Aegean, there is a Mycenaean settlement at Poliochini; Melos in the Cyclades, has a prehistoric settlement at Phylakopi, where there are three successive cities, the earliest dating to the third millennium B.C. and the latest to the end of the Mycenaean period.

Santorini, a volcanic island, is situated on the edge of an old volcano and is famous for the discoveries made by Professor Marinatos at Akrotiri. These revealed a whole city stretching from one side of the island to the other. It was a Minoan settlement, with marvellous frescos and was destroyed during a devastating volcanic eruption in c. 1500 B.C., which caused the destruction of the whole island and began the vast tidal waves that devastated the north and east coasts of Crete, causing destruction to Knossos, Phaistos, Mallia and Ayia Triada.

Rhodes in the Dodecanese, was settled first by the Achaeans when they dominated the Aegean with their navy, setting up trading posts on the coasts of Asia Minor, Syria and in the Greek islands. Later the island was dominated by the Dorians, under their leader Neoptolemus, who had taken part in the Trojan War and who settled in Rhodes c. 1100 B.C.

In Greece, before the advent of archaeology, the primary source of knowledge of the past was the Homeric poems, to which were attached a whole series of epics dealing with the Trojan War. Although Homer in the *Iliad* confined himself to certain episodes in the tenth year of the war, the journey of Odysseus on his way back from the Trojan War, is the subject of Homer's other epic poem *The Odyssey*. Homer tells how many of the Greek gods took part in the war, on one side or the other. Thus Athene, Hera and Poseidon fought on the side of the Greeks and Apollo, Ares and Aphrodite on behalf of the Trojans.

After Homer comes Hesiod, who attempted to synthesize the legends in his *Works and Days* and *Homeric Hymns*. These were intended to set out, in blank verse, the genealogical side of tradition, which is to say the descent of families from gods or heroes and the *Theogony*, the account of the gods and their struggle with the giants telling "how at the first gods and earth came to be . . . and how at the first they took many folded Olympus".

Following Hesiod came the story-tellers, whose object was to give the earlier legends in prose form, completing them and adding names where they were missing. One of the best known of these was Hecataetus of Miletus, an Ionian site on the coast of Asia Minor, which had originally been a Mycenaean settlement.

Certain areas in Greece were richer in legends than others, such as Argolis, Boeotia, Thessaly and Attica. Some legends were local, others extended their influence over the whole of Greece, like those of Heracles and Jason and the Argonauts. In Athens, during the Classical Period, the legends served as a source for Greek plays by such authors as Sophocles and Euripides, who changed the legends still further and they often have different versions or different endings. It was not until the writings of Herodotus of Halicarnassus in Asia Minor, that Greek history was placed on a firm basis but one must remember that the Greeks themselves believed implicitly in their legends and regarded them as factual.

In Medieval Greek stories, memories of earlier legends survive but they have suffered changes over the years and although they may have the same names as deities or nymphs in Classical stories, they are no longer the same. Up to the end of the last century, particularly in the northern provinces still subject to the Turks, in Albania, Thessaly and Macedonia, there were many pagan survivals. Many of the folk songs refer to Charon, the boatman of Hades but now he appears more in the guise of a messenger who removes the souls to the Afterworld. He also wrestles with the souls but they are never known to win.

5

II

The Beginning of the World

Many of the early legends about the beginning of the world commence with chaos and those of Greece are no exception. The Ancient Greeks believed that after chaos was born the goddess Gaea 'Wide bosomed Earth, the sure foundation of all'. The earth was, according to Hesiod, a flat disc floating upon a waste of waters surrounded by the river Oceanus. The creation of Earth was followed by that of Eros, not the young god of love as known in the later tradition but a primeval being 'fairest among the deathless gods'.

Gaea bore Uranus 'the starry heaven', who became Gaea's partner. There was never a cult of the sky as such, so Uranus receives no recognition although Gaea continued to be worshipped throughout Greece until the end of the Historic Period.

After Gaea, other deities came from chaos such as Erebus, black night and Aether, the atmosphere. The children of night who came from chaos were Doom and Black Fate, Death, Sleep and Woe, also the Hesperides who guard the apples on the edge of the Western World, Destiny and Fate, as well as Nemesis, Deceit, Age, Strife and Friendship.

Gaea and Uranus had twelve children known as the Titans, six male and six female. Among them were Oceanus, Rhea who replaced her mother as Earth Goddess, and Cronus 'the Wily' who was to replace his father Uranus. After the Titans, they bore the Cyclops, giants with one eye in the centre of their foreheads. These were followed by three monsters with fifty heads each and numerous arms, who, with the Cyclops, were sent to Tartarus.

Oceanus the Sea God, bore many children, the eldest being Nereus whom men call 'the Old Man of the Sea'. Nereus had fifty daughters who were skilled in crafts; one of these was Thetis, mother of Achilles and one of his granddaughters was Iris 'Winged Messenger of the Gods' whom we meet later.

The twelve Titans were hated by their father Uranus, who wished to destroy them for he feared they would otherwise destroy him, so Gaea hid them underground for safety. Eventually, Uranus was reduced to impotence by Cronus, who ruled in his place and liberated his brothers and sisters from the earth. Cronus married his sister Rhea but alarmed by an oracle that said he too would be supplanted by one of his sons, he swallowed each one as soon as they were born. Rhea, displeased, turned to Gaea and Uranus for help, and on their advice, went to Crete before the birth of her last son, having given Cronus a stone to swallow instead of the baby. This child, Zeus, was born in a cave on Mount Aegeum or Mount Ida in Crete and was brought up by Gaea, fed on goats' milk and sweet-scented honey and given to the nymphs of the mountain for safe-keeping.

The oracle that had said Cronus would be overthrown by his own son, was correct. When Zeus reached manhood he decided to punish his father and called Metis, a daughter of Oceanus, to his aid. She gave Cronus a draught which caused him to vomit up the stone that Rhea had substituted for Zeus, followed by all his other children he had swallowed. Then Zeus supplanted his father and with his brothers and sisters lived on Mount Olympus where they became gods instead of Titans. The other Titans, with the exception of Oceanus, were jealous of the new gods and wished to regain control of the world. They lived on Mount Othrys and from there they launched fierce attacks on Mount Olympus. Zeus descended into Tartarus where the Cyclops and other monsters born of Gaea and Uranus had been imprisoned. He freed them and enlisted their help.

The struggle between the Gods and the Titans went on for ten long years. The Cyclops gave Zeus thunderbolts and he burnt the forest with lightning and the earth was ravaged by the war. Finally, the Titans, including Cronus, were overcome and were cast into the depths of the earth.

The difference between the various Titans is not clearly defined but the Ancient Greeks honoured them as the ancestors of man.

Hardly was the war over with the Titans than a fresh peril threatened the gods. This came from the giants who had sprung from the blood of Uranus. They attacked Olympus and by heaping Mount Ossa on Mount Pelion (still a well-known saying) for a scaling ladder, they almost reached the top of Mount Olympus. The gods grouped round Zeus and had great difficulty in withstanding the attack but with the aid of Heracles, the giants were finally defeated. However, Gaea could not quite reconcile herself to her children losing power and sent a monster, Typhon, to fight Zeus. It finally succumbed to Zeus's thunderbolts and fled to Sicily to live under Mount Etna.

Zeus fighting the monster Typhon.

All this time the elements were in wild disarray, the earth writhed and shook under vast earthquakes and the sea boiled as volcanoes rose from the depths. Eventually, when all was calm, the gods withdrew to Mount Olympus.

III

The Olympians

Mount Olympus is in Northern Greece on the border between Macedonia and Thessaly. It rises to a height of 9,500 ft. and the summit is perpetually wreathed in cloud; the slopes are wild and rugged, wooded with many streams. Here the gods lived, in splendid marble palaces decorated with fabulous paintings. It was always summer and the gods, who never aged, forever feasted on nectar and ambrosia, listening to the strains of sweet music played by Apollo on his lyre and the songs of the birds. After mankind was created, the gods had to be propitiated with burnt offerings and libations. They frequently took part in mortal quarrels, one against the other. The gods were like humans in many respects, subject to the same likes and dislikes, loves and hates, but unlike mankind, they were immortal. 'Ichor' instead of blood flowed in their veins and though they could be wounded they could never be killed.

There were twelve gods and goddesses on Olympus: Zeus, Poseidon, Hephaestus, Hermes, Ares and Apollo, Hera, Athene, Artemis, Hestia, Aphrodite and Demeter. Hades, though one of the great gods, did not frequent Olympus, so he is not listed among the twelve. Besides these were some earlier deities who did not relinquish their pride of place like Helius, the Sun God, Selene, the Moon Goddess, Leto, Dionysus, the God of Wine and Themis. Then there were those who served the gods like Iris, the messenger, Hebe, who served them ambrosia, the Graces, the Muses and Ganymedes, the cup-bearer.

Zeus was the king of the gods and his symbol as a Sky God was a thunderbolt. His brother, Poseidon, ruled the sea and all water, and was known as 'the earth-shaker' as he was associated with earthquakes (Greece being in an area where they occurred

Zeus, father of the gods.

frequently). Poseidon was also the master of horses and had a horse-drawn chariot. When he travelled on the sea, he had a chariot drawn by Tritons, who were half-men, half-fish. He lived in a splendid palace beneath the waves and is represented as a mature, bearded man. The third brother, Hades, ruled the Underworld, the home of the dead, a dark forbidding place from which no one returned. It was encircled by the rivers Acheron, Lethe and Styx and guarded by the three-headed dog, Cerberus. However, above the gods was an even more powerful being, to whom all were subject. This was Moros, or Destiny, one of the sons of Night. Even Zeus could not go against his will; all had to obey him.

Zeus had many wives, the first was Metis, Wisdom, by whom he had Athene, Goddess of the Home and also a warrior goddess. Forewarned by Gaea and Uranus that if he had children by Metis they would become more powerful than he was, a fear that always seemed to haunt the gods, he swallowed Metis and the unborn Athene to avoid this happening. Zeus suffered terrible headaches as a result and to relieve them, Hephaestus, the God of Fire, split open his head with a bronze axe and from the wound sprang Athene, fully armed and carrying a spear. Zeus, next married Themis, a goddess of the earth, symbolizing law and order. She was a most respected goddess and remained Zeus's adviser even after she had been superseded by Hera. The children of Zeus and Metis were the Horae (Seasons), Dike (Justice), Eunomia (Order) and Eirene (Peace). A Titaness, Mnemosyne (Memory) also married Zeus, to whom she bore nine daughters, known as the Muses. Another wife was Leto, who had the twins, Apollo and Artemis from him. Zeus also had many children by nymphs, oceanids and mortals. His last wife was Hera, who became his queen. She was a sky goddess and became the Goddess of the Hearth, Home and Marriage. Their children were Hebe, who served the gods, Ares, God of War and Eileithyia, Goddess of Childbirth. Hera was a very jealous goddess, not without reason, and tormented her rivals in various, ingenious ways.

One of Hera's sons was Hephaestus, presumably born before she married Zeus. He was lame and ugly, disliked by his father and forever quarrelling with his mother. He once took revenge on her by building her a marvellous golden throne which had invisible bonds. Hera, on receiving the gift, promptly sat down on it but when she tried to get up found she was held firmly in place. The other gods tried to help her but without success. Hephaestus, being the only one who could release her, hid in the sea and refused to return to Olympus. At last after Ares had failed to bring Hephaestus back, Dionysus made him drunk, put him on the back of a mule and drove him back to Olympus. Hephaestus was still adamant about not releasing Hera and would only agree to do so if Zeus gave him the most beautiful of the goddesses, Aphrodite, as his wife. After that incident, his relations with his mother improved, but not those with Zeus. Zeus was so irritated by his son's interference in his quarrels with Hera that he flung him out of Olympus.

Having been flung out twice, Hephaestus eventually landed on Lemnos and was said to reside under Mount Moschylus, a volcano, where he was worshipped. Later he was thought to have migrated to Sicily to live under Mount Etna. The gods were unwise to have thrown Hephaestus out as he was the God of Craftsmen and Fire, particularly connected with terrestial fire and volcanoes. He built the gods' palaces and the furniture to go in them, including Zeus's golden throne, so was very useful to them. He worked in metal for gods and for men, thus he made the armour of Achilles and the golden goblet given to Aphrodite. No job was too small for him. He helped Zeus on more than one occasion; he constructed Pandora to please him and tied Prometheus to a crag in the Caucasus. Traditionally, Hephaestus was trained as a blacksmith in Naxos. He was helped by various genii and the Cyclops, not the one-eyed giants that met with Odysseus but the sons of Gaea and Uranus, who had been thrown into Tartarus and saved by Zeus but were later killed by Apollo, in revenge for killing his son, Asclepius.

Like most of the other gods, Hephaestus's love life was complicated and unsatisfactory. He was married to Aphrodite, the Goddess of Love, who was continually unfaithful to him, not only with Ares but also with Hermes. Nor did she confine herself to divine beings but fell in love with Anchises, a Trojan shepherd by whom she had Aeneas, the founder of Rome. Aphrodite took over the role of Astarte and was loved by Adonis in Phoenicia. She also appears in Anatolia where she takes the guise of the moon goddess, Silene and wooed Endymion, a shepherd. The site of this myth is Heracleia under Latmos, on the shore of Lake Bafra in Caria.

IV

The Coming of Man

According to Hesiod's *Work and Days*, there were five Ages of Man. It it not known the exact order or in which age the legends and stories fit. Pandora's jar and the flood may come after the Silver Age but the majority of legends probably come from the Bronze and Iron Ages. The first age was the Golden Age, when man was free from all toil and sickness and lived happily on the fruits of the earth. This was followed by the Silver Age, when man was far less noble, failed to make sacrifices to the gods and so was destroyed. The third age was that of Bronze, when man devoted himself to fighting with bronze weapons and again was destroyed by the gods. The fourth age was that of Iron and is the age before that in which we live. It was the time of the heroes and demi-gods, many of whom were destroyed by war and battle. Some fought at Troy for Helen's sake, others released from war, lived untouched by sorrow in the Islands of the Blessed. Along the shore of the deep swirling ocean, Cronus, released from his bonds by Zeus, ruled over them. Hesiod says "Far-seeing Zeus made yet another generation of man, who are upon the bounteous earth . . . and men never rest from labour and sorrow by day and from perishing by night and the gods shall lay sore trouble upon them . . . Strength will be right and reverence shall cease to be; and the wicked will hurt and the worthy man, speaking false words against him . . ." This is the fifth age that is still with us.

MANKIND

Iapetus, a Titan, married Clymene an Oceanid, and they had four sons. Two of them, Menoetius and Atlas, were punished by Zeus for having sided with the Titans in the struggle against the gods. For his audacity, Menoetius was plunged into darkest Erebus, south of chaos, and Atlas was compelled to stand forever on the borders of the western world, holding on his shoulders the vault of the sky. Later, he was turned to stone and became the Atlas Mountains. The other two sons, Prometheus and Epimetheus, had remained neutral in the struggle and as a result, Prometheus had even been admitted to Olympus. However, he was not altogether on the Olympian side as he resented what had happened to the other Titans. He therefore resolved to create a new race of beings which he hoped would counteract the power of the gods. With the help of Epimetheus, he created mankind out of clay, but he was unable to endow them with life and had to ask Athene for help. This she readily gave and breathed life into the clay figures. The reputed site for this miracle was Phosis.

PANDORA'S JAR

Zeus was angry with mankind, so he called Hephaestus and asked him to make a woman, so perfect that she resembled the gods in form. He called her Pandora, but although she was beautiful she was irresponsible. She was sent to Epimetheus, who had been warned by his brother Prometheus, never to accept any gifts from the gods as it would bring trouble. However, when Epimetheus saw Pandora, he fell in love with her and forgot all about the warning. Pandora had brought with her a sealed jar which was inscribed 'Not to be Opened'. This Pandora longed to do as she was sure it must contain a nice present. So one day, unable to withstand the temptation any longer, she opened the jar. Immediately the air was filled with the noise of fluttering wings and all the diseases that mankind would suffer from flew out and dispersed. Pandora hastened to close the jar, but it was too late. All that was left was the spirit of Hope, which Zeus had included, so that however dark things would appear, mankind could still cling on to the hope of something better.

THE GREAT FLOOD

It would have been wise for mankind to have propitiated the gods but they did not always do so and Zeus was displeased when he found some men had turned to cannibalism. So as to punish them, he sent a great flood. First the sea rose up over the shores, then the rivers overflowed their banks so that there was no land left except the tops of the highest mountains. At this time the son of Prometheus was living upon earth. He was called Deucalion and was warned by Prometheus of what was going to happen. His father told Deucalion to build an ark and to get inside it with his wife, Pyrrha, the daughter of Epimetheus and Pandora. For nine days and nine nights the ark floated on the waters until it came to rest on Mount Parnassus, in Central Greece. Deucalion thought they were the only survivors and hastened to make sacrifices to the gods (so they must have had animals with them) at a ruined shrine to Themis, the Goddess of the Earth and of Justice. He implored the goddess to restore mankind. The oracle instructed them to cover their heads and to cast the bones of their mother behind them. This, Deucalion interpreted as the stones of the earth, 'Mother of All'. So they picked up some stones and the ones that Deucalion cast behind him turned into men and those that Pyrrha cast behind her turned into women. Thus was mankind restored.

At a meeting of gods and man to determine what offerings should be made to the gods, Prometheus was placed in charge of the sacrifice of an ox. He arranged the carcass into two parts, made two bags out of the hide and in one placed the bones, topping them with a thick layer of fat and in the other he placed the flesh and entrails. Zeus had the choice and misled by the fat on the top, chose the one with bones which caused him to fall into such a rage that he denied mankind the use of fire. Prometheus knew well that they could not get anywhere without fire so he stole a brand of fire from Olympus and hiding it in a stalk of fennel, gave it to mankind. Zeus was so furious that Prometheus had helped man that he ordered Hephaestus to seize Prometheus and bind him with indestructible chains, to one of the mountains in the Caucasus. There an eagle, some say a vulture, tore at his liver all day. There was no end to his pain as his liver grew again each night, only to be attacked the next day. Eventually Zeus relented and Prometheus was released.

THE STORY OF EUROPA

This story tells how Europe got its name. Europa was the daughter of the King of Tyre, a town on the Phoenician coast, now the Lebanon. One day while she was playing near the sea-shore collecting flowers with her maidens, Zeus saw her and thought her rather attractive. He turned himself into a magnificent white bull and came and grazed among the herbage near her. He was so beautiful that she approached and stroked him, he knelt down and for fun she mounted his back and placed a wreath of flowers around his horns. Immediately he rose up and plunged into the sea, swimming until he reached the south coast of Crete, at a place called Gortyna. Here Europa bore him three sons, Minos, who became King of Cnossus, Rhadamanthus and Sarpedon, thus beginning the Cretan royal line. Asterius, King of Crete, later married Europa. A plane tree at the place where Europa and Zeus lived in Crete became divine and many years later was shown to Theophrastus when he visited the island. It was said never to shed its leaves because it had once sheltered a god. Europa is traditionally held to be the ancestress of all Europeans.

The abduction of Europa.

V

Hermes

The derivation of the name Hermes is uncertain. It has been suggested that it is connected with a word for a stone or rock. Certainly he was often worshipped in the form of a stone, the *herm* or *hermai*, not as statues of him but square pillars of stone which tapered towards the bottom and had a phallus half way up the front. Hermes was probably a Pre-Hellenistic god belonging to the old Pelasgian deities.

Born in a cave on Mount Cyllene in Arcadia, Hermes was the son of Zeus and Maia, a daughter of Atlas. Like many of the gods, he was precocious from birth, as indeed were his half-brothers Apollo and Heracles. His first act was to steal the cattle which Apollo was supposed to be caring for. He took fifty heifers and drove them to the banks of the Alpheus. After sacrificing two of them to the gods of Olympus, he went back to his cave, disguising his footprints by making sandals from myrtle and tamarisk and then pretended he had never been out. Apollo did not notice the theft until the following day but when by divination, he discovered that Hermes was the thief, he went straight to the cave. There Maia showed him the child safe in his cradle. Hermes denied the theft but Apollo, furious, took him before Zeus, who though amused at the child's antics, ordered him to give back the animals. They went to the banks of the Alpheus where Apollo was charmed by the music Hermes played on his lyre. He had made it from an empty tortoise shell; it was seven stringed and said to be the first lyre made in Greece. Hermes gave it to Apollo and, in exchange, Apollo gave Hermes a golden wand, the prototype of the Caduceus, the winged staff Hermes carried as the messenger of the gods. He also gave Hermes the care of the cattle instead of himself. Thus it

Hermes, the messenger of the gods.

was that the two became firm friends and as a result, Apollo became the God of Music and Hermes the Protector of Flocks and Herds.

As the messenger of the gods, Hermes was the protector of travellers and trade. He was represented as a young man with winged feet, winged helmet and the Caduceus. In his form of messenger, he was connected with athletic contests and became the God of Games. His image was set at crossroads and along difficult paths and he was said to conduct the souls of the dead to the Underworld. Hermes was a very popular god and crude stone images of him were placed by the Greeks, in front of their doors. He had festivals throughout Greece called the Hermea, when offerings were made of incense and cakes, and pigs, lambs and goats were sacrificed there. The palm tree, tortoise and certain fish were sacred to Hermes.

Hermes undertook many important missions for Zeus, though his sense of fun sometimes got the better of him. He put Argus, the watchman with a hundred eyes, to sleep with the aid of his music, then killed him. He helped to free Zeus when he was taken captive by Typhon, the monster, and he released Ares from captivity. Hermes helped the Heroes carry out their feats, accompanied Heracles to Hades and encouraged Perseus in his struggles. He had numerous children by goddesses and nymphs, the best known of whom was Pan.

VI

Demeter and Persephone

Demeter, the daughter of Rhea and Cronus, was also an earth goddess, particularly concerned with the harvest and fertility of the earth. She was worshipped in Greece, Asia Minor, especially in Lydia, and in Sicily, which had been colonized by the Greeks and is the setting for the following story.

Demeter had a daughter, by Zeus, called Persephone or Kore which means child. She was so beautiful that everyone loved her and thought of her as 'spring personified'. She used to spend long, happy days in the fields helping her mother to polinate the flowers and gather the corn. Now Hades, the ruler of the Underworld, was lonely and one day whilst visiting the earth in his swift chariot, he heard the sound of merry voices and laughter. He quickly drew rein and stepped down parting some bushes to see who was there. At once he saw Persephone, in the middle of a ring of young girls who were pelting her with flowers. Hades was delighted with her and said to himself, that girl will make a splendid queen for me. He knew it was no use asking for her consent for who would want to live in the underworld before they had to. So he consulted his brother Zeus and with his encouragement, snatched Persephone and carried her off in his chariot.

To avoid being seen with her, he took a roundabout route home. All went well until he reached a stream where the water nymphs, furious at what they saw him doing, stirred up the waters so that the stream became a raging torrent, which he was unable to cross. However, what is the use of being a god if one cannot overcome difficulties and so he struck the ground with his sceptre, whereupon the earth opened and he passed through it to his kingdom. Persephone, realizing that the water nymphs had recognized her, took off her girdle and flung it as far as she could, just as the earth was closing over her, in the hope that her mother would see it and know what had happened to her.

When Demeter got home that night, Persephone was not there and no one could tell her where she was. So Demeter took up her cloak and carrying in her hand a torch that she had lit at Mount Etna, searched everywhere for her. On the tenth day she met Hecate, one of the goddesses of the Underworld, who told her what had happened. Demeter went straight to the Sun God Helius, who sees everything that takes place on earth, to ask him if what Hecate had said was true and if Persephone was really in the Under-world. Helius told her that Zeus had given her to Hades for his wife and that Hades had taken her away, crying, in his chariot. Demeter was seized with anger, particularly with Zeus, and know-ing that no one ever came back from the Underworld was filled with sadness and grief.

Demeter avoided the assemblies of the gods on Olympus and remained on earth. She went to the house of Celeus and Metaneira where she became nurse to their son, Demophoön. Under her guardianship the child grew strong and healthy. Every night she anointed him as though he were a god and he grew more beautiful by the day. She also used to place him in the fire so that when all that was human had burned away he would become an Immortal. One day his mother chanced to see this and screaming with fear made Demeter take him out. The goddess told Metaneira, "Humans are witless and if you had left me I could have made your son immortal like the gods, but now he cannot escape death and the fates. Yet shall unfailing honour be with him because I nourished him and held him in my arms, for I am Demeter, the great goddess. Now build me a temple upon the hill of Callichorus and I myself will teach the people the rites". When she had spoken the goddess resumed her true shape and cast age from her, her golden tresses spreading around her shoulders so that the whole house was filled with brightness. Celeus called all the people to him and straight away they built a temple to Demeter on the hill, and placed her altar within.

Still Demeter mourned the loss of her daughter Persephone and in her anguish caused a most dreadful year to come upon man-kind. The earth could not make the seeds sprout, the land was ploughed and the seed sown but to no avail. She would have dest-royed all mankind with a terrible famine had not Zeus intervened. Zeus sent Iris, the messenger of the gods, to see Demeter who was waiting in her temple in Eleusis. Iris called her to a council of the gods on Olympus, but Demeter was stony-hearted and would not listen. Then the other gods and goddesses visited her and asked her to attend the council but still Demeter refused, saying she would not set foot on Olympus or let fruit and grain spring out of the ground until she beheld Persephone again. On hearing that, Zeus sent Hermes to the Underworld to ask Hades to let Persephone see her mother so that her terrible anger with the Immortals and man-kind should cease. Reluctantly, Hades agreed and gave Persephone a pomegranate to take with her as she was weak with hunger, hav-ing eaten nothing all the time she had been in the Underworld.

Hermes took her, in his golden chariot, back to her mother and Demeter rushed to embrace her daughter. Even as she did so, she feared a trick and anxiously asked Persephone if she had eaten anything while she was in the Underworld because if she had not, she would not have to return to Hades. Unfortunately, Persephone, being very hungry, had eaten three seeds of the pomegranate, which resulted in her having to return to the Underworld for three months of each year. Demeter declared that for those three months, the earth would be cold and dark but when she returned to earth it would be spring and the flowers, birds and all living things would rejoice until the time when she had to return once more to her husband. Zeus then ordered Demeter to join the gods and goddesses and sent Rhea to fetch her. Demeter was comforted and caused the grain to spring from the earth again and the fruit and grain to grow. Mankind was saved and Demeter went to Olym-pus to sit with Zeus among the gods as was her due.

VII

The Birth of Apollo and Artemis

Zeus had two children by Leto, Apollo the God of Light and Music, and Artemis the Great Huntress. When Leto was pregnant, Hera, who was very jealous of her, chased her from place to place, never allowing her to settle anywhere long enough for the children to be born. Finally, Leto came to an island called Ortygia, which was under the guardianship of her sister Asteria and protected by Poseidon, who threw a wall of water over the island to hide Leto. There her twins were born, first Apollo and then his sister Artemis. The island now known as Delos, which means 'brightness', became one of the most important of Apollo's shrines to which people came from far and wide.

Apollo and Artemis with their mother Leto.

LETO AND THE FROGS

After the children were born, Leto was driven out of Delos by Hera and wandered for a long time in dry and stony places on the Asiatic mainland. There were no trees or bushes and no water, and her feet were burnt on the hot sand. The two children, whom she carried in her arms, seemed to get heavier and heavier, whilst the sun shone evermore fiercely on her with its burning rays. It seemed that she had been walking forever when suddenly she saw a clump of trees and a glimmer of water nearby. Relieved, she hurried towards the place, in the hope of getting something to drink. When she got there, she found a beautiful lake of clear blue water round which there was a fringe of reeds, which some men were plucking. Leto tried to bend down to get a drink but could not do so as she was clasping both the children. As she put them down she was surprised to hear one of the men order her not to drink. "Why not?" said Leto. "Surely you will not forbid me to drink of the water which has been put here for everyone." But the men threatened her and said that if she did not go away they would attack her. Leto pleaded with them to at least allow the little ones a drink but instead of answering her, the men began to throw stones and mud into the water until it became quite undrinkable. Then Leto got very angry, for as you know it is unwise to offend the gods. She raised her head to heaven and called on Zeus to help her and asked that these men might forever live in the pool. Zeus heard her cry and the men were at once changed into frogs. To this day they haunt the quiet pool, now sitting on the rocks, now leaping into the water and filling the air with their harsh cries.

APOLLO

Fed on ambrosia after his birth, Apollo developed rapidly and soon became very strong. He needed to as he had to kill a serpent called Python, which Hera sent to plague Leto and the twins. This monster serpent lived on the slopes of Mount Parnassus and whilst looking for a place to establish his shrine, Apollo had wandered into the gorge where Python lived, and was attacked by the monster. With the arrows given him by Hephaestus, Apollo was able to

24

shoot the monster. The place was at first called Pytho after the serpent but later became Delphi and here Apollo erected his shrine. Not surprisingly, no one was living on Mount Parnassus so he could not find anyone to serve his shrine. He solved the problem by capturing a Cretan ship sailing in the gulf by transforming himself into a dolphin and making the sailors his priests. As a result Apollo became the protector of sailors and the god of navigation.

To purify himself after killing Pytho, Apollo went to the Vale of Tempe in Thessaly and later returned to Delphi crowned with laurel, which became his emblem. A festival to commemorate these events took place at Delphi every nine years, called the Septeria, in which Apollo was portrayed by a youth who re-enacted the ritual of burning down a wooden hut which represented Pytho's lair. After this the youth would make a pilgrimage to the Vale of Tempe and return to Delphi amid great rejoicings.

How Apollo obtained the laurel as his emblem is yet another story. He was always represented as a young man in the first flush of manhood and naturally he had many love affairs, many of them unhappy. He fell in love with a nymph, Daphne, the daughter of the River God Peneius. As she did not want anything to do with Apollo, she fled from him. When he ran after her and was about to catch her, she called on the Earth Goddess Gaea for help and the earth opened up and swallowed her. Out of the hole into which she had disappeared sprang a tree; it was a laurel, which Apollo adopted as his emblem.

Another unfortunate love affair Apollo had, was with Cassandra, daughter of King Priam of Troy. In return for her favour, Apollo conferred on her the gift of prophecy and the power of foreseeing the future. However, as she did not keep her side of the bargain, Apollo asked for a single kiss and breathing upon her, took from her the ability to make her prophecies sound convincing, so no one would believe her.

Apollo was an excellent archer and he thwarted the attempts of two of the giants, Ephialtes and Otus, to reach Olympus by piling Ossa on Pelion by shooting them down with his arrows. He also killed the giant Tityus, son of Gaea; a favourite theme on Greek vase paintings. He sometimes attacked men but only with good reason, as when he killed with a single blow, Phorbas, a strong man who waylaid travellers and killed them on their way to the shrine at Delphi. He even fought with Heracles, when Heracles disappointed that the oracle at Delphi refused to prophecy for him, stole the Sacred Tripod. Zeus had to intervene to separate them.

Several of Apollo's friends came to an untimely end. The youth Cyparissus was changed into a Cypress tree because he was broken-hearted after killing a favourite deer but the best known of these stories is that of Hyacinthus. One day when he and Apollo were throwing the discus, Boreas and Zephyrus, who were jealous of Hyacinthus, blew the discus thrown by Apollo off its course. It struck Hyacinthus on the forehead and killed him. Out of the blood that gushed from the wound grew up a purple flower, the hyacinth, and when the wind blows through them it repeats his name over and over again, Hyacinthus, Hyacinthus . . . As a result of his death, a festival called the Hyacinthia was held every year in Laconia, which began with lamentations and funerary offerings and changed to songs of gladness in memory of the young prince, who at his death had become one of the Immortals.

THE MUSES

As God of Music, Apollo was greatly honoured on Olympus. His lyre was given to him by Hermes and he was attended by the nine Muses, who were the goddesses of poetic inspiration, music and poetry. Their cult originated in Thrace where festivals in their honour were held every five years. In Athens, a hill near the Acropolis was consecrated to them and they were worshipped at Delphi, Thrace and elsewhere in Greece. They were young women in long flowing robes and each carried the symbol of her attributes. Thus Clio, the Muse of History, carried a trumpet and a clepsydra; Terpsicord, who was the Muse of Lyric Poetry, carried a cithara and Urania, the Muse of Astronomy, had a globe and compass. The Muses were, according to Hesiod, the daughters of Zeus and the Titaness Mnemosyne, which means memory. Although they went to Olympus and took part in the Immortals' festivals, they preferred to remain on earth and live on the slopes of Mount Helicon in Boeotia, where there were woods and many springs. They also went to Mount Parnassus, where there was the famous spring of Castalia, whose waters were supposed to give poetic inspiration. Like all the gods, they were extremely jealous, especially of mortals who claimed to excel in one of their arts. For instance, they struck dumb and blind a Thracian bard, Thamyris, who claimed his skill was superior to theirs, while the daughters of King Pierus, who made the same claim with regard to poetry, were turned into magpies. Occasionally they married, although most of them remained single. Thus Calliope, the Muse of Epic Poetry, married Oeagrus and their son was Orpheus, the celebrated singer.

ARTEMIS

Artemis was a great huntress who lived in Arcadia. She is said to have asked her father Zeus for a bow and arrows and a short hunting tunic. She hunted, accompanied by sixty Oceanids and twenty nymphs, who looked after her pack of hounds. She took another form in Asia in which she was an early mother goddess. One of her maidens, Callisto, was loved by Zeus and as a result had a boy, Arcas. Artemis, when she heard that Callisto had a small child, was furious as she thought that all her nymphs should devote themselves only to hunting. She therefore turned Callisto into a bear and for many years Callisto wandered about the woods in a shaggy coat, eating nuts and wild honey, avoiding all contact with human beings. After some fifteen years she was surprised by her son Arcas, in a forest glade; he had, in the meantime, become a very fine hunter. She recognized him, even after all those years, but of course he did not recognize her and was just about to shoot her when Zeus intervened and snatched the bow from his hands. For Zeus still loved Callisto and would not allow her to be killed by her own son. To make up for her life as a bear, he placed both Callisto and her son in the sky, where they shine at night as the Great Bear and the Little Bear.

THE TEARS OF NIOBE

Now Thebes in Boeotia was a strong and powerful city ruled over by a king and queen. The queen's name was Niobe and they had fourteen children, seven boys and seven girls. When they were young, Niobe would love to play with them and dried their tears if they were miserable. As they grew up, she still remained devoted to them. Every spring there was a great festival held in Thebes in honour of Leto and her two children, Apollo and Artemis. It was particularly a woman's festival, and women brought garlands and offerings, such as cakes and honey to the temple in honour of Leto. One year when the women were on their way to the temple, they met Niobe, splendidly dressed, who said to them, "Why do you worship Leto when I am more powerful and as for her children, mine are far stronger and more beautiful? Stop worshipping Leto and make your offerings to me instead, for I have far more than Leto ever had". This alarmed the women and instead of going to the temple and making their sacrifices, they flung down their wreathes at the door of the temple and hurried home in silence.

Leto heard what went on as she had come to the top of the mountain overlooking Thebes in order to see the festival held in her honour. She particularly liked to hear the hymns sung to honour herself and her children. The sort of hymns that were sung were as follows: "I will begin with the Muses and Apollo and Zeus. For it is through the Muses and Apollo that there are singers upon earth and players upon the lyre; but kings are from Zeus. Happy is he whom the Muses love; sweet flows speech from his lips. Hail children of Zeus! Give honour to my son". (*Homeric Hymns*, XXV). On this day there were no hymns. Leto, hurt and wounded, hastened to find Apollo and Artemis to tell them how Niobe had boasted she was more powerful than the gods and that nothing could harm her.

Now Apollo and Artemis were very fond and proud of their mother and when they saw how upset she was they hastened to calm her. Veiled in clouds to hide their radiance, they hastened to Thebes to avenge her. There, they found the seven princes exercising their horses and Apollo swiftly shot them all down with his arrows, starting with the eldest. The terrible news quickly reached the palace and Niobe rushed out, followed by her seven daughters. But she was not yet humbled and raising her arms she cried aloud, "I am still greater than you are Leto for I still have seven daughters and you have only one". This was too much for Artemis who grasped her bow and hastened to shoot down Niobe's daughters. Niobe tried to save the last one by hiding her in her cloak, then called upon the gods to spare her one. Too late, even the youngest child fell shot at her feet. Then Niobe sat down among her dead children and neither moved nor spoke but wept continuously. Finally, she wept so much that she was turned to stone, a marble pillar

Apollo and Artemis slaying the children of Niobe.

standing on the plain outside Thebes, until at last it was swept by a storm into the mountains, where it lay above a spring. The inhabitants of the area call the spring, Niobe's fountain, as they believe the water to be Niobe's tears, still falling.

VIII

The Story of Io

In a remote part of Greece, there was a beautiful grove of trees through which ran a small river tumbling down the hillside to reach the sea. The god of the river had an only child, called Io, of whom he was very fond. There was nothing that Io liked better than to wander in the grove by her father's stream. One day when Zeus was strolling about the earth, disguised as a man, he met Io and thought her very attractive. As time went on, he spent more and more time with her, which, of course, was noticed by Hera who was very jealous of Zeus paying attention to anyone except herself. When he had been absent from Olympus rather longer than usual, Hera decided to go and see what he was doing. By this time, she was very angry and when she reached the grove where Zeus and Io were, she was frowning deeply. Zeus could feel his wife's approach and immediately turned Io into a cow so that when Hera arrived, all she saw was her husband and a white cow cropping herbage. She knew at once that the cow was Io and she went up to her and said what a beautiful animal she was and could she please have it as a present. This was rather awkward for Zeus who did not wish to give her the cow, could think of no excuse not to, so he did.

Hera led the cow away and placed it in the care of one of her servants, Argus. Argus was an excellent watchman, who had one hundred eyes and only fifty of them went to sleep at any one time. Never for a moment was Io left unguarded and at night she was tied to a tree. Poor Io did not understand what had happened. Instead of the food to which she was accustomed, she now had to eat grass; she could no longer speak and could only utter plaintive moos. Even the water nymphs, her former companions, did not know her. Furthermore, her father failed to recognize her and she was devastated. Argus, who was worried in case she might find

30

some way of communicating with her father or the nymphs, drove her to a place far away from home and sat down on top of a near-by hill to watch over her.

Meanwhile, Zeus had not forgotten Io and sent Hermes, the messenger of the gods, with orders to kill Argus. Hermes flew down to earth, dressed as a simple shepherd and collected some stray sheep to complete the picture. He had brought his reed pipe with him and began to play it. Argus was quite pleased to see him as it was rather boring watching Io all day, so he asked Hermes to sit beside him and tell him some stories. Hermes sat down beside him and played on his pipe and told him stories but Argus never went to sleep and never closed more than fifty of his eyes at one time. Eventually, Argus asked Hermes where he had got his pipe and Hermes told him the following story:

"Once there was a nymph called Syrinx who lived in the for-est. She used to play with the other nymphs and satyrs and was a very swift runner. One day Pan, who was the god who protected shepherds, flocks and herds, and had the head and body of a man and the ears, legs and feet of a goat, and was the chief of the satyrs, came to visit the part of the woods where Syrinx was. He had never seen her before, so went over to speak to her, but she was frighten-ed by his goat's ears and goat's legs and she ran away so fast that Pan could not overtake her. At last she reached a stream and here she called on her sisters, the water nymphs, for help. They heard her cry and reached up and drew her down into the water. On the bank where she vanished, appeared a clump of reeds. Pan who arrived soon after found these instead of the nymph he was seek-ing. He breathed a deep sigh and his breath among the reeds made a soft murmuring sound like music. Pan was charmed and cutting a handful of reeds, he glued them together with wax and made a musical pipe that he called Syrinx in honour of the missing nymph."

Hermes told the story in a very sleepy voice and made it last as long as he could and was delighted to see when he had finished that all of Argus's eyes were shut and he was sound asleep. Hermes did not waste any time in cutting off Argus's head and took it back to Olympus to show Zeus. Hera was furious and most unfair-ly blamed Io for the death of Argus. She set his one hundred eyes in the tail feathers of the peacock, her favourite bird, where they have remained ever since. Thereupon, she sent a large gadfly to torment Io. The gadfly bit her by day and by night until she became nearly demented. She wandered from country to country with no respite. Finally she reached Egypt where she lay down by the banks of the Nile and called on the gods to relieve her sufferings. Whether it was because the writ of the Greek gods did not hold sway in Egypt or because the Egyptians had a powerful cow goddess, Hathor, Io regained her own shape and was later worshipped in the land to which she had come.

IX

Heracles

Heracles was born in Thebes although his family came originally from Tiryns. Officially his father was Amphitryon and his mother Alcmene but his real father was Zeus, who had visited Alcmene in the guise of her husband. Heracles had a twin, Iphicles, who was the son of Amphitryon. The goddess Hera was extremely jealous of Alcmene and of Heracles, the son whom she bore to Zeus, despite his name Heracles being compounded with her own. It meant 'Glory of Hera' and throughout his life she pursued him with vengeance. Whilst he was still in the cradle, she sent two snakes to attack him and though Iphicles ran away, Heracles strangled them. Heracles had many masters to train him. Amphitryon taught him to drive a chariot, Autolycus taught him wrestling, Pollux fencing, Eurytus archery and Linus music. The last had disastrous consequences, as Heracles, more of a sportsman than musician, killed Linus with his own lyre, having lost his temper when reprimanded. Heracles escaped prosecution for this murder by pleading self-defence. However, he was sent off to guard the cattle pasture of Amphitryon, his education being deemed complete.

At the age of eighteen, he killed a lion on Mount Cithaeron, which was preying on the herds of Amphitryon. On his way to Thebes, after this episode, he fell in with messengers of Erginus, King of the Minyans of Orchomenus, who were coming to collect the tribute of Thebes. Heracles cut off the ears and noses of the messengers and hanging them round their necks, sent them back to Erginus with a message that he would get no other tribute. Not unnaturally, Erginus was furious and attacked Thebes, but Heracles backed by Athene, who gave him weapons, and assisted by the Theban army, defeated the Orchomenians and forced them to pay a double tribute to the Thebans. Creon, King of Thebes, was delighted and gave Heracles his daughter, Megara, in marriage. At first all went well and Heracles and Megara lived happily together, until Hera remembered her feud with Heracles and sent upon him a fit of homicidal madness during which he killed not only Megara but his children. After this crime, Heracles had to go into exile to work off his blood guilt. He became a servant of Eurystheus, King of Tiryns, for twelve years. It was the Delphic Oracle that sent Heracles to the King of Tiryns and also told him that only after he had completed twelve labours for the King would he be purified.

Meanwhile, Heracles married Deïanira, daughter of King Oeneus of Calydon, brother of Meleager, the hero of the Calydon boar hunt. Deïanira went with Heracles to Tiryns. On the way, they came to the river Euenos in flood, which she could not cross. Nessus, a centaur, offered to help her across then tried to rape her; for this, Heracles shot and killed him. As he lay dying, he told Deïanira to take some blood from his wound so that if ever Heracles should prove unfaithful, she was to smear some of it on a garment, give it to him to wear and it would cause him again to fall in love with her. She accepted his friendly advice and safely kept some of the centaur's blood. This story is undoubtedly out of sequence as the point of it was that the centaur Nessus was killed by Heracles with arrows that had been tipped with the poisonous blood of the Hydra, which was the second labour of Heracles.

The Labours of Heracles

Traditionally there are twelve labours, in some of them Heracles is assisted by his nephew, Iolaüs, the son of his twin brother, Iphicles. The labours are as follows:

1.   *The Nemean Lion*

Hera had sent a lion to the region of Nemea where it ravaged the surrounding territory. The lion lived in a cave with two exits and was invulnerable because of its very tough hide, which no weapon could pierce. When Heracles shot at it with his arrows they glanced off. He then tried to hit the lion with his club but to no effect. He finally approached the lion and strangled it with his bare hands. When the animal was dead, he flayed it and ever afterwards was seen wearing the lion skin, which made him, like the lion, invulnerable. When Heracles brought the lion's body back to the King of Tiryns, Eurystheus, was so alarmed that he bade Heracles leave anything else he should bring back outside the city. The Lion of Nemea was commemorated by Zeus, who placed it in the sky as a constellation.

2. *The Lernean Hydra*

The Hydra was a monster, the offspring of Echidna and Typhon. It was a kind of dragon with multiple heads whose venomous breath killed everything within reach. It was especially reared by Hera as a test for Heracles. The Hydra lived near Lerna in the Peloponnese; its den was in the marshes from which it used to venture forth destroying all within reach. In this labour, Heracles was assisted by Iolaüs without whose help he would have been unable to subdue the beast. Iolaüs set fire to the marshes and drove out the Hydra but every time Heracles cut off one of the Hydra's heads, it grew back again. Eventually, with Iolaüs's help, Heracles was forced to cut it off and bury it. He then dipped his arrows in the Hydra's blood, which made them poisonous.

3. *The Wild Boar of Erymanthus*

In this labour, Heracles was to bring back alive a large boar that lived on Mount Erymanthus. It was winter time and the ground was covered with thick snow. Having driven the boar from its lair by loud shouts, Heracles chased the boar through the snow until it became exhausted. He was then able to net it and take it back to Eurystheus. While hunting the boar, Heracles came across the centaur, Pholus, the son of Silenus and a nymph. He was hospitably received by Pholus and offered cooked meat. When he asked for wine to accompany it, he was told that there was only one jar of wine, which belonged to the community of centaurs. Heracles insisted on opening it but no sooner had the scent of the wine pervaded the air than centaurs began arriving from all directions. Instead of sharing the wine, Heracles killed the first two centaurs to

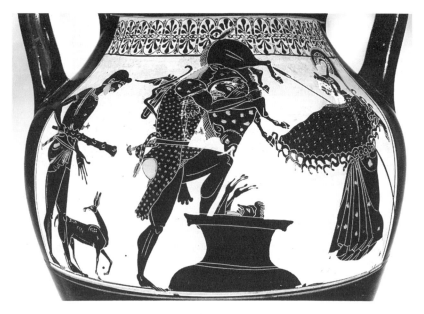

Heracles bringing the boar to Eurystheus.

arrive and destroyed many of the others, including Pholus, who while burying one of the centaurs, drew out one of Heracles's poisoned arrows and accidentally dropped it on his foot. The centaurs fled to Cape Malea, where they took refuge with Cheiron on Mount Pelion. Cheiron was the wisest and most famous of the centaurs, the son of Cronus and the Oceanid, Philyra, and he trained many of the Greek Heroes in the arts, sciences and arms. Heracles who had followed the centaurs, shot Cheiron and wounded him on the knee with one of his poisoned arrows. Cheiron, who was immortal, found the wound would not heal because it contained the blood of the Hydra. He suffered greatly and exchanged his immortality with Prometheus and was therefore able to die.

4.   The Hind of Ceryneia

The hind was sacred to Artemis, so that Heracles had to hunt the hind but was not permitted to kill it. It took Heracles a whole year to find it and he finally came on the animal while it was asleep and ensnared it. On the way back to the Argolid, Heracles met

Artemis and Apollo, and Artemis asked for her hind back. Heracles agreed but asked for permission to show it to Eurystheus first, and then he released it.

5. *The Stymphalion Birds*

There was a lake at Stymphalus in Arcadia, the borders of which were densely wooded. It had become a perfect bird sanctuary and was thickly populated with birds who had fled there to escape the depredations of wolves in the surrounding countryside. As a result, the birds became a menace to the area, feeding on the fruit and crops. Eurystheus ordered Heracles to destroy them. Heracles got Hephaestus to make him a rattle, or castenets, the noise of which drove them out of their coverts so that he could easily shoot them down.

6. *The Stables of Augeias*

This was an attempt by Eurystheus to humiliate Heracles by forcing him to undertake a menial task. He was told to clean out the stables of Augeias, King of Elis (one of the Argonauts), who had vast herds of cattle, whose stables had never been cleaned, so that huge piles of dirt had accumulated. Heracles demanded in payment, one tenth of the herd if he cleaned the stables in one day. Augeias readily agreed as he thought the task impossible. Thereupon Heracles took down one wall of the stables and diverted the rivers Alpheius and Peneus through them, to wash away all the dirt. However, Augeias refused to keep his side of the bargain and was later punished by Heracles for this. Heracles also ran into difficulties with Eurystheus, who claimed he had received payment for his labour so that it could not be counted as one of the twelve tasks.

All these first six labours are centred round the Peloponnese, but with the next tasks the scene of action is further afield.

7. *The Cretan Bull*

Traditionally this was a bull which rose out of the sea off the island of Crete, after the king, Minos, had promised to sacrifice to Poseidon anything that appeared from the sea. However, Minos was so delighted with the handsome bull, that he decided to sacrifice an inferior animal to Poseidon, placing the bull from the sea in his own herd. The god, infuriated, made the bull untameable and it was this animal that Eurystheus asked Heracles to bring back. Minos refused to co-operate but gave his permission for Heracles to capture the bull if he could. This Heracles managed to do, catching it alive and then taking it to Eurystheus, who was far too nervous to touch it. Eventually Heracles let it go and after wandering about for some time, the bull settled in the plain of Marathon in Attica.

8. *The Horses of Diomedes*

Diomedes, King of the Bistonians, was a son of Ares. He owned a herd of horses, whom he was accustomed to feed on human flesh. Heracles was required to bring the horses to Eurystheus. Opinions vary as to whether he did this task alone or, because of the difficulties involved, had volunteers to assist him. The story goes that Diomedes died in the ensuing round-up and was fed to his horses, which effectively tamed the steeds. Heracles, then, took them to Argos where they were dedicated at the shrine of Hera.

9. *The Girdle of the Queen of the Amazons*

The Amazons were legendary female warriors who lived somewhere in Asia Minor, on the borders of the known world, where it shades from reality to legend. The Queen of the Amazons was called Hippolyte and she had a girdle that had special powers. Eurystheus required Heracles to obtain it for him (Apollodorus says that it was his daughter who wanted it) as it had magical qualities that made it especially appealing. After various adventures, Heracles arrived at the land of the Amazons where he either defeated the Amazons and was offered the girdle by Hippolyte or, more likely, he killed her to obtain it. The story is told in connection with a relic, said to be the actual girdle, shown in the temple of Hera at Argos, in classical times.

10. The Cattle of Geryon

Geryon was a monster with three heads, who lived far away in the lands of the west, on the island of Erythia (Red Island) in the stream of the Ocean, a mythical island, a fairyland realm lost in the glow of the sunset. Geryon had a splendid herd of cattle, guarded by his herdsman, Eurytion and his dog, Orthros. Eurystheus ordered Heracles to go to the island and bring him back the cattle. The first problem was how to cross the sea and to do so Heracles had to borrow the golden cup of Helius and put to sea in that. Buffeted by the waves of the ocean, Heracles threatened Oceanus, one of the gods of the sea, with his arrows and the waves subsided. Once he arrived at the island of Erythia, Heracles killed the dog Orthros with one blow of his club. He then dealt the herdsman a death blow and made off with the cattle. Geryon, who had been absent when all this was going on, immediately followed Heracles to the banks of the river Anthermos and here he was shot down by Heracles.

On his return journey, Heracles had several adventures in the Western Mediterranean. On one occasion, he briefly passed into the Atlantic Ocean and to celebrate his passage he erected two columns, one on each side of the strait separating Africa from Europe, known hereafter as the Pillars of Heracles. In Calabria, one of the bulls escaped and swam across the sea to Sicily. Whilst recovering the bull, Heracles left the rest of the herd in the care of Hephaestus. Meanwhile, Eryx, a Sicilian hero, tried to capture the bull but he too was killed by Heracles. When they finally arrived back in Northern Greece, the herd was attacked by gadflies, sent by Hera. As a result, the animals scattered all over the place and Heracles had great trouble in rounding them up. At last, his journey complete, Heracles turned over the surviving bulls to Eurystheus, who sacrificed them to Hera.

11. The Golden Apples of the Hesperides

When Hera married Zeus, Gaea the Earth Goddess gave her three golden apples as a wedding present. These, Hera placed on the Tree of Life in her garden, far in the west, near Mount Atlas.

The tree and the apples were under the guardianship of an immortal dragon, who had one hundred heads, the child of Typhon and Echidna. Three nymphs of the evening, the Hesperides, also guarded the tree, and it was these three golden apples that Eurystheus sent Heracles to fetch. Heracles had a difficult journey to reach the garden. First of all he crossed Libya where he had to wrestle with a huge bandit called Antheus, son of Gaea, who drew his strength from his mother, the earth. The only way Heracles could defeat him was by holding him up, so that he was not in contact with the earth, and then strangling him. Heracles also passed through Egypt where he is said to have visited Busiris, in the Delta, the city of Osiris. Here he slayed the king whose habit it was to sacrifice every foreigner that passed that way. For some reason, he then went to Ethiopia and Arabia where he killed Emathion, and climbed the Caucasus to free Prometheus. Prometheus told him that he could not obtain the apples without the help of Atlas, a giant who bore the whole weight of the sky on his shoulders.

Heracles finally arrived at the land of the Hyperboreans where he found Atlas. He offered to relieve Atlas of the weight of the sky if he went to collect the golden apples for him. This Atlas did but, on his return, he told Heracles that he wanted to take the apples to Eurystheus. Heracles pretended to agree to this proposition but asked Atlas to take the weight of the sky for a moment while he got a cushion to protect his shoulders. Atlas took the weight but as soon as Heracles was relieved of the burden, he picked up the apples and fled away. However, Athene did not consider the apples suitable for mankind and returned them to the Tree of Life.

12. *Heracles and Cerberus*

Despairing of ever giving Heracles a task that would defeat him, Eurystheus finally instructed him to descend to Hades and return with Cerberus, the three-headed dog who guarded the Underworld. Guided by Hermes, the messenger of the gods, and assisted by Athene, Heracles descended the path of Taenarum. When the Dead Shades saw him they fled before him. Eventually, on reaching Hades, he asked the gods permission to take away

Cerberus. Permission was granted, provided Heracles mastered the dog with his bare hands, without recourse to weapons. After a fierce struggle wrestling with the dog, he eventually overcame it and took it back to Eurystheus, who promptly took refuge from the dog in a brazen jar. Heracles then returned the animal to his rightful post as guardian of the Underworld.

These last two labours have been considered by some as attempts to obtain immortality for Heracles. After completing all the tasks, Heracles carried out a number of campaigns against various kingdoms and had many adventures. Everywhere he went, fighting seems to have broken out. Finally one of his adventures led to his death. Tiring of Deïanira after many years of marriage, he was promised the hand of Iole, daughter of King Eurytus of Oichalia, if he won an archery test. This he did with ease but the king refused to carry out his part of the bargain. In a rage, Heracles killed the king's son, Iphitus, by casting him from the ramparts of Tiryns. Once again, Heracles went to Delphi to have Apollo purify him from his blood guilt but the Pythia, the priestess of Apollo who gave out the oracles, refused to speak to him. Angered, Heracles stole the sacred tripod from Apollo's sanctuary, causing a quarrel with Apollo, which dragged on and on until Zeus was forced to intervene. The oracle was finally persuaded to speak and condemned Heracles to a year's slavery to King Eurytus with no wages.

However, in the end he did marry Iole and this led to his downfall. Deïanira remembered what the centaur Nessus had told her many years before, that if she feared she was losing Heracles, love would be renewed by giving him a garment dipped in the centaur's blood. Knowing that Heracles needed a new tunic for a sacrifice he was to make to Zeus, she dipped the garment in the blood she had kept safely over the years. Warmed by the sacrifice, the poison in the blood became active and Heracles was unable to tear off the tunic which stuck to his skin. In great pain, Heracles decided to commit suicide and climbing Mount Oeta, he built a funeral pyre there. When all that was mortal of Heracles had burnt away, the divine portion was raised in a cloud to Mount Olympus, where he was finally reconciled to Hera, made an immortal and married to Hebe, the personification of youth.

X

The Argonauts and the Search for the Golden Fleece

The myth of the Argonauts had its origins in Thessaly in Northern Greece, but was famous throughout the country. The story interlocks with that of Ino, daughter of Cadmus, who hated her stepchildren Phrixus and Helle. After she threatened their lives, they fled on a golden ram, who could fly and talk. Helle fell off and was drowned in the Hellespont but Phrixus continued as far as Colchis on the Black Sea in Southern Russia. There he sacrificed the golden ram to Zeus, such is human gratitude, and gave the fleece to the king, Aeëtes, who nailed it to an oak tree in a wood dedicated to Ares. There it remained for many years guarded by a dragon who never slept. The object of the voyage of the Argonauts was to recover the Golden Fleece.

In Thessaly, Pelias had overthrown and killed his half-brother Aeson but had been warned by an oracle to beware of a man with only one sandal. Aeson's son, Jason, was rescued by his mother and given to Cheiron the Centaur to be brought up and educated with the other princes he taught.

When Jason was fully-grown, he returned to Thessaly to reclaim his kingdom. On the way, he stopped to help an old woman across a stream and in so doing lost a sandal in the mud. The old woman was really the goddess Hera in disguise and from then on, she always supported Jason. Upon seeing Jason with only one sandal, Pelias remembered the oracle and decided to send Jason on a mission from which he hoped he would never return. Thus was Jason set the task of fetching the Golden Fleece.

Jason began by asking Argus, the son of Phrixus, to build him a ship. The vessel, named *Argo*, had fifty oars and a prow constructed of a special oak from Dodona, which had the power of speech. The *Argo* was built at Pagasae, the port of Iolcus, where the re-

The building of the 'Argo'.

mains of a Mycenaean settlement had been found. The crew he
gathered to go with him became known as 'the Argonauts'; among
them were the fathers of the heroes of the Trojan War, such as
Peleus, father of Achilles, Telamon, father of Aias, and Laertes,
father of Odysseus. Others were the heroes who took part in the
Calydonian boar hunt, including Meleager himself, Laocoön, his
father's brother, and Atlanta, the only woman on the expedition.
There were also representatives from various Greek states, like
Theseus of Athens and others who were obviously added later,
such as Orpheus and Heracles. Tiphys was the helmsman until he
died in the land of Mariandyni and was succeeded by Erginus.

The *Argo* sailed from Pagasae calling at Lemnos, an island they
found to be inhabited only by women (see the Nemean Games).

Here they remained for a year and would probably have stayed longer if Heracles had not persuaded them to move on. They had a brief stop at Chios as Heracles had broken an oar and it was here, his page Hylas was seized by water nymphs when he went to get some water from a spring. Heracles refused to continue the voyage without him and remained on the island searching for the boy. It has been suggested that Hylas was originally a fertility deity connected with vegetation, as on the orders of Heracles, the people of Chios went on searching for him every year, only stopping in the spring with the new growth of vegetation.

The Argonauts' next difficulty was the Symplegades or Clashing Rocks, which stood at the entry to the Black Sea. They were moving reefs, which clashed together every time anything tried to pass them. The Argonauts were advised to release a dove and if it got through unharmed, to follow it. The dove managed to do this, losing only a few tail feathers as the rocks clashed together. The *Argo* followed, only receiving slight damage to her stern. Traditionally, the rocks then remained stationary, as fate decreed that once a ship had passed through them unharmed, they could no longer move.

Having arrived at the Black Sea, the Argonauts sailed to the land of the Mariandyni, where the king, Lycus, received them favourably. During a boar hunt, the seer Idmon was wounded and subsequently died; here too, the helmsman Tiphys died. The Argonauts proceeded on their way, skirting the Caucasus and finally arriving at the mouth of the river Phasis in Colchis (modern Rhioni in Georgia).

Jason began to negotiate with King Aeëtes for the return of the Golden Fleece. Aeëtes eventually agreed to give it to him provided he met certain conditions. First, he had to yoke, unaided, two bulls with brazen hooves, who breathed fire, which had been given to Aeëtes by Hephaestus. Then he was to plough and sow a field with dragon's teeth. This was the dragon killed by Cadmus, which Aeëtes just happened to have in his possession. In reality, of course, Aeëtes had no wish to give up the Golden Fleece as, in some way, it was linked to the fate of his city.

Jason would never have succeeded in this task had he not had the help of Medea, the king's second daughter, who was an enchantress and had fallen in love with Jason and wished to return with him to Greece. She gave him balm which made him invulnerable to iron and fire; she also told him that from the dragon's teeth would spring forth armed men who would try to kill him unless he threw a stone among them. Thus forewarned, Jason managed to plough the field, sew the dragon's teeth and from a distance, cast a stone among the warriors and those that did not kill one another, he slew. Meanwhile, Aeëtes tried to burn the *Argo*, but before he could do so, Jason managed to detach the Golden Fleece from the tree on which it was hanging, as Medea had put a spell on the dragon that was guarding it.

There are varying accounts of the return voyage of the *Argo*. Most agree the journey was long and difficult. Aeëtes pursued the ship and would have caught them had not Medea, who was with the Argonauts, killed her younger brother and cut up his body, scattering the pieces along their course, thus slowing the progress of Aeëtes, who tried to recover the bits. The *Argo* sailed as far as Scylla and Charybdis, off Sicily and the Wandering Isles. Eventually they arrived back at Iolcus. Pelias was by now an old man and Medea soon disposed of him by telling his daughter that he could be rejuvenated by putting him in a cauldron of hot water containing special herbs. At the last moment, she changed the herbs and made the water so hot that Pelias was boiled alive. This was too much for Acastus, the son of Pelias, and he drove out Jason and Medea. They went to Corinth and there, after many years, Jason grew tired of Medea and cast her off. He wanted to marry Glauce, daughter of King Creon but he had not reckoned on Medea's jealousy. She sent the bride a robe smeared with a burning agent which destroyed her and also her father when he tried to save her. Thereupon, Medea escaped to Athens in a winged chariot, whilst Jason remained in Corinth, a rather sad and lonely figure. He dedicated the *Argo* to Poseidon and would go and sit in its shade and meditate on the voyage, until the day a timber from the decaying ship fell upon him and killed him.

The legend of the Argonauts is best known to modern readers from Apollonius's Rhodos *Argonautica*. It is also interesting to note that in Svanetia, a mountain area in the Caucasus, where gold is found and which used to be the prime source of gold for Colchis, the ram was a sacred symbol. Colchis was famous for its gold in the Ancient World. The miners would gather the gold from the streams that come down from the mountains fed by the melting snows. They would place in the waters, sheepskins with the fleece uppermost, nailed flat on wooden platforms and weighted so they lay on the bed of the streams. As the water flowed over the fleeces, gold, being heavier than sand or silt, became trapped in the wool. Indeed, in the upper reaches of the streams, the fleece becomes so impregnated with gold that it appeared like a golden fleece. Doubtless, the origin of the legend. Soviet archaeologists have since found confirmation of the legend, in the discovery of a temple, sacred to bull worship, and guarded by snakes. For snakes, read dragons, as the two were often interchangeable. This evidence was uncovered by Tim Severin when he sailed to Soviet Georgia in a modern replica of the *Argo*, with a mainly British crew in the summer of 1984.

XI

Orpheus and Eurydice

Orpheus, the Greek master-singer, was the son of Apollo and the muse, Calliope. His home was in Thrace and he was renowned, not for being a warrior but for his musical prowess. He sang and played the lyre with such sweetness that the very beasts of the field were enchanted.

At the request of his mother, he was trained by the centaur, Cheiron, on Mount Pelion. Among his companions being taught with him to hunt, ride and wrestle, was Heracles, famed for his labours, Peleus, who was to become famous as the father of the hero Achilles, Asclepius who spent his time wandering through the forest gathering herbs and samples and who was to become the greatest healer in Ancient Greece. It was here too, that he met and made friends with Jason.

Orpheus accompanied Jason on his quest for the Golden Fleece. It was his singing that was supposed to have made the ship *Argo* slip from her position high on the beach, where she was built, into the water. When the terrible rocks, the Symplegades, threatened to crush the *Argo* between them, it was his music that was said to have stopped them and sent them down to the bottom of the sea. He was also supposed to have lulled the dragon which guarded the Golden Fleece to fall asleep, by singing so sweetly, and his final effort on the voyage was to prevent the sirens from attacking the Argonauts.

Orpheus fell in love with a nymph, Eurydice, whom he found playing with her sisters by a mountain stream. It was love at first sight; they married and lived in the woods in a hut made of twisted branches where they lay on bundles of dry grass. None of the animals would ever hurt them as they all loved and respected Orpheus and his wonderful lute. However, their happy life came to a tragic end when Eurydice was bitten by a snake whilst fleeing from Aristaeus, the Thessalian Pan, a primitive deity and son of Uranus, who had also been brought up by Cheiron.

Orpheus was in despair and went to the Underworld, determined to rescue Eurydice. He took his lute and descended to the dark regions by the cave of Taenarum, in the south of the Peloponnese. When he reached the river Styx, his music charmed Charon, the ferryman, who took him across the river in his boat. Once in the Underworld, he was able to charm Hades and Persephone and they agreed to release Eurydice and let her return with him, on condition that on the journey back he must not look behind him. The couple had almost reached the outer gate of the Underworld, when Orpheus, anxious that Eurydice was not following him, turned his head and instantly, Eurydice was whisked back to Hades.

Orpheus looking back at Eurydice when she returns from the Underworld.

Orpheus was inconsolable. Some say he died of grief or that he killed himself. Others say he was torn to pieces by the Thracian women. His lyre was supposed to have been in the temple, on Lesbos, and was too sacred for anyone to touch. Here too, his head came to rest and an oracle of Orpheus existed there in later times.

XII

The Contest of Poseidon and Athene

This is a very old myth, whose origins lie in the Mycenean citadel and palace on the Acropolis of Athens. The area is now occupied by the Erechthion, a temple built at the end of the fifth century B.C. It contained three symbols or tokens: a well of salt or brackish water, a mark on the rock said to have been made by a trident and the sacred olive tree, which grew within the precincts.

The story goes that Poseidon and Athene strove for the possession of the Land of Attica. Both deities created gifts for the people of Attica; Poseidon made a well of salt water by striking the rock with his trident. Some say when he struck the rock the first horse ever to have been seen in Greece appeared. Athene, on the other hand, touched the rock with her spear point and an olive tree appeared. Her gift was judged by the people of Attica to be the more valuable and Athene became the patron deity of Athens. The marks of Poseidon's blow can still be seen, even today, within the porch of the Erechthion, which has an opening left in the floor and in the roof above, so that the sky is always visible. Poseidon was so furious at losing the contest that he flooded the Thracian Plain. Only when the other gods intervened, were Athene and Poseidon reconciled.

Poseidon was worshipped as Poseidon Erechtheus, a title behind which lies a link with the mythical ruler, Erechtheus, who may well have symbolized an early Mycenean ruler. The salt spring was still being shown to visitors at the time of the Emperor Hadrian, A.D. 117-138, and the sacred olive was still alive at the time of Herodotus, in spite of attempts by the Persians to burn and destroy it.

This legend of the contest between Poseidon and Athene is only one of many, concerning Poseidon. At Argos he strove with

Athene.

Hera for possession of the city and lost, whereupon he promptly flooded the surrounding countryside. When the flood subsided, a temple to Hera was built on the spot. At Troezen, Poseidon contended with Athene but as no solution could be found, Zeus judged that they should both receive equal honours.

The Athenians, however, had made a wise choice, as Poseidon was a very temperamental god, whereas Athene was just and served the city well.

XIII

Theseus of Attica

King Aegeus of Attica was childless so went to consult the oracle at Delphi, which promised him a child after he had returned home. On his way back, he went to Troezen in the Peloponnese to consult King Pittheus. Here he fell in love with the king's daughter, Aethra. It is interesting to note that Aegeus being an eponym of the Aegean Sea, so Aegeus is a local form of Poseidon. Anyway, in due course a son was born to Aethra. He was named Theseus. Before the child was born, Aegeus returned to Athens leaving behind him, his sword and sandals, which he placed under a heavy rock with instructions that when the child was old enough to lift it and get the sword and sandals, he was to join his father in Athens.

When Theseus was sixteen, his mother told him about his father and showed him the rock he had to lift. Being brave and strong, he easily managed to lift it and retrieve his father's things. Instead of going straight to Athens by sea, he chose to go over-land as it offered him more adventures. Near Epidaurus, he killed the brigand Periphetes and took away his terrible club with which he used to kill travellers. He, thereupon, killed Sinus, the pine bender, who tied his victims to two stretched pine trees which when released tore them apart. Theseus meted out the same treatment to him. Next he hunted and killed the grey sow of Crommyon, which was devastating the surrounding country. In Megaris, a district between the Corinthian and Saronic gulfs, he met another brigand, Sciron, who used to kick people into the sea as they washed their feet. Theseus flung him into the sea in retribution. After further adventures from which he continued to emerge victorious, he arrived at Athens.

Meanwhile, Aegeus had married Medea who was jealous of Theseus as soon as she saw him and tried to poison him. Theseus

Theseus lifting rock to take his father's sword.

drew his sword, which Aegeus recognized immediately, and Medea was turned out. Aegeus had been continually having trouble from Pallas and his sons, who were trying to seize the throne and overthrow him. Theseus, however, soon disposed of them. His next act was to catch the Marathonian bull, the one Heracles had brought from Crete, which was laying waste the surrounding countryside.

At this time, Athens was under the subjection of King Minos of Crete because of the murder of his son, Androgeüs, in Attica. Among the terms imposed upon Athens was a yearly tribute in the form of seven youths and seven maidens to be sent to Knossos where they were shut in the Labyrinth, where they either died of hunger or were eaten by the Minotaur. Theseus chose to go as one of the youths in the hope of killing the Minotaur. He made an arrangement with his father that if he was successful, he would raise a white sail on his vessel when he returned, instead of the black sails that were used in mourning for the youth of Attica.

On their arrival in Crete, Ariadne, the daughter of King Minos, fell in love with Theseus. She gave him a sword and a thread which by unwinding behind him, enabled him to find his way back through the Labyrinth after killing the Minotaur. Theseus and his companions sailed for Athens taking Ariadne with them but left her behind on the island of Naxos. In some accounts, Ariadne is depicted not as a princess but a goddess who befriended Theseus. Deserted, Ariadne was found by Dionysus, who married her. The constellation in the sky, Corona, is identified with the girdle Dionysus gave her. Although Theseus had promised to change the sails to white if he were successful in killing the Minotaur, he forgot to do so and Aegeus, keeping a look-out on the cliffs at Sounion, saw the black-sailed vessel approaching, and thinking his son to be dead, flung himself off the cliffs and was drowned.

Theseus now became king of Athens and instituted various reforms, the most notable of which was the union of the scattered Attic communities into one, centred in Athens. Here history touches upon legend, as this really happened. He had many more adventures and went on the Voyage of the Argonauts. However, Theseus's difficulties were not over; Athens was invaded by the Amazons, a tribe of women warriors from Asia, who had been provoked by the campaign that Heracles, with the support of Theseus, had waged against them. Theseus managed to defeat them and married their queen, Hippolyte, sometimes known as Antiope, by whom he had a son, Hippolytus.

After the death of Hippolyte, Theseus married Phaedra, a sister of Ariadne. She, however, fell in love with her stepson and when he repulsed her, she hanged herself, leaving a letter incriminating Hippolytus. Theseus banished the boy but on his way into exile, the horses were frightened by a sea monster and he was thrown from his chariot and killed. Too late, Theseus realized the truth. Saddened by tragedy, and rebellions against him, Theseus took refuge on the island of Skyros, where he died or was possibly murdered by Lycomedes, the king of Skyros.

There is no doubt that Theseus is a purely legendary character, although the Athenians regarded him as an historical figure.

XIV

Meleager of Calydon

Meleager was the son of the king of Calydon. The three Fates, Clotho, Lachesis and Atropos, came to his naming. Clotho foretold he would be a great hero, Lachesis that he would inherit great strength and Atropos forewarned that his life would last as long as the piece of wood that was burning on the fire. When his mother, Althea, heard this, she immediately snatched the log from the fire, plunged it in water and kept it carefully knowing that her son's life depended on its preservation.

When Meleager grew up, all the things foretold by the Fates took place. He was one of the heroes that sailed with Jason on the *Argo*. His courage saved his country from many misfortunes, but he is chiefly remembered, in legend, for hunting the great Calydonian boar. At the great Harvest Festival of the year, Meleager's father sacrificed to Demeter, grain and barley cakes, to Dionysus, wine, and to Athene, olive oil, the produce of the tree she had given to Greece. To all the other gods and goddesses he sacrificed what was right and proper. However, he forgot one very important goddess, Artemis, and had left her altars bare of offerings. As you know, the gods are very jealous and Artemis was no exception. She was very angry and sent a boar to ravage the fields around Calydon. It was a huge animal with large tusks and the very sight of it was enough to send panic into the stoutest heart. It trampled down the corn, savaged the standing crops and tore up the vines just as they were fruiting and then turned its attention to the flocks and herds. Even the fierce, farm dogs with their iron-spiked collars were savaged, and the country people had to take refuge within the city walls to save their lives.

To fight this scourge, Meleager assembled a band of young heroes all anxious to win renown. These included many of those who had sailed with him on the *Argo*. Nestor, then a young man, Jason, Castor and Pollux, Peleus, father of Achilles, Laertes, later to be father of Odysseus, Theseus of Athens and his friend Pirithoüs. There were not only men, as Atlanta the huntress also came along. Meleager was attracted by her but as he had a great deal to do, entertaining all the heroes, he had little time for dalliance.

The boar had its home in a forest which ran up the slopes of the mountain, an area which had never been cleared so the trunks of the trees stood very close together. Here, the hunters assembled with their dogs and nets. They eventually found the boar at the foot of the mountain, in a small valley filled with willows, sedge, bullrushes and reeds. It rushed out of its lair, scattering the hunters and uprooting trees and bushes as it went, plunging into the dense forest where they could not follow on their horses. They shot arrows at it but Artemis intervened to protect the boar so that most of the heroes' weapons missed their mark, except for Atlanta's arrow which slid along the boar's back, piercing its neck behind its right ear.

Meleager was as delighted as if he had drawn the first blood himself, but the others were rather put out and began to boast and shout. Then one of them, Ancaeüs, took a large double-headed axe and running in front of the rest, shouted how much better a man's weapons were than a woman's. But as he stood with upraised axe, poised to kill, the boar tore him to pieces with its tusks, his boasting, to no avail. Jason missed the boar with his javelin, pinning instead one of the hunting dogs to the ground. Meleager's first spear drove into the boar's back, then he plunged his second spear through the boar's shoulder and finally killed it. Even when it was dead, the hunters could hardly believe how large and ferocious it looked. Meleager put his foot on its head and said to Atlanta that as she had been the first to wound it, she should have the prize and presented her with the skin and the head with its huge tusks. The other hunters were not pleased, and his two uncles, brothers of his mother Althea, shouted at Atlanta to put down the prize as it belonged to men not girls. They also deprived Meleager of the right to dispose of the prize. Meleager was furious and turned on Plexippus, the nearest uncle, shouting that deeds spoke louder than words and that he had no right to take what belonged to others and stabbed him through the heart with his sword. While his other uncle, Toxeus, hesitated about what to do, Meleager turned on him and killed him also.

Back in the city, Althea was bearing gifts to the temple to celebrate her son's victory when she saw the bodies of her two brothers being carried in for burial. She ripped off her golden robes of celebration, put on black and cried and beat her breast with grief. When she heard that the murderer was her own son, she remembered the log that held his fate. She ordered a fire to be lit with pine shavings so that it would burn quicker. Then she hesitated as she could not decide what to do for the best, whether to kill her son in revenge for his uncle's murder or save him because he was her son. Finally her love for her brothers won the day and she cast the log on the fire. Mealeager, far away in the forest and ignorant of what was happening, suddenly felt himself burning all over. He cried for help to his father and sisters but in vain. As the log burnt, so did he and as it died away to ashes, his soul left his body. The whole of Calydon went into mourning for Meleager; his old father lay down and died, his sisters mourned him with loud cries and burnt his body on a splendid funeral pyre. His mother, unable to bear the grief and the guilt for what she had done, stabbed herself to death. Thus ended the royal house of Calydon.

XV

Atlanta's Race

Atlanta was a huntress, very beautiful and a fast runner. When she consulted an oracle as to whom she should marry, Apollo replied: "Do not take a husband, Atlanta, for if you do it will bring disaster upon you". Afraid of this prophecy, Atlanta withdrew to the woods and remained unmarried. There was no lack of suitors for her hand but she always had only one answer for them. This was "No one can have me for his wife unless he can beat me at running. If you so desire, I will race with you and if you win I will be the prize, but if you lose, you will forfeit your life". But even with these cruel terms, there were many young men anxious to race against her.

One day a young man called Hippomenes came to watch one of the races, though not to take part. He had always thought young men who raced against Atlanta quite mad, but that was before he had seen her. When he did see Atlanta, he fell in love with her and, naturally, wished to compete for her hand also. Atlanta did not wish to run against him as she thought he was too young, but he insisted. Hippomenes prayed to Aphrodite to help him. Now it so happened that the goddess heard his prayer and was moved by it. She had just returned from her island, Cyprus, where in the garden of one of her temples grew an apple tree which bore golden leaves and golden fruit. She had gathered three apples, which she brought with her. So she descended to the earth, invisible to all, except Hippomenes, and showed him how to use the apples.

When the signal to start the race was given, Atlanta soon outran Hippomenes, who was left panting and distressed. Then, remembering the goddess's instructions, he threw the first of the golden apples in front of her but at an angle, off course. Atlanta saw the

Aphrodite, goddess of love.

60

gleaming fruit and sped after it. As she stopped to pick it up, Hippomenes ran past her. Very soon Atlanta made up the time and overtook him. The same thing happened when he threw down the second apple; again he was soon overtaken. He threw the last apple at a sharp angle from the course and Atlanta hesitated over whether she should go after it. However, Aphrodite who was anxious to see the outcome of the race, prompted her to do so. When Atlanta picked up the apple, Aphrodite made it weigh heavily in her hand, thus handicapping her. This time she failed to catch up with Hippomenes, who won the race.

On claiming Atlanta as his wife, Hippomenes forgot that he owed his success to Aphrodite. He neither thanked her nor offered her the rightful sacrifices. As you know, the gods got very jealous if their due rights were not observed. Aphrodite was, therefore, furious and resolved to make an example of the pair. On their return to Hippomenes' home, they passed a temple sacred to Cybele, the great mother goddess, imported into Greece from Asia Minor. This was a sacred spot, forbidden to all but the initiated. However, Aphrodite encouraged them to stop and rest within its sacred precincts as they were tired from their journey. This deeply offended Cybele, and in the middle of the night, she visited them and turned them into a lion and a lioness, compelled forever to dwell in the savage woods and be at Cybele's behest to draw her chariot whenever she wished. Thus was Atlanta's fate fulfilled.

XVI

Arachne's Web

One of the twelve great deities of Olympus was Pallas Athene, the daughter of Zeus and Metis. Pallas Athene was the protector and patron goddess of Athens, probably a pre-Hellenic goddess, which would account for her martial characteristics. She was a warrior goddess in her form of Athene Ergane and the guardian of the Athenian Acropolis. Born fully armed and brandishing a javelin, she was always represented as a mature woman wearing a helmet and holding a spear and shield. She was also the goddess of handicrafts, particularly of weaving. She was a moral and righteous deity, but like the other Greek gods, she could sometimes be unreasonable. In Athens she had three temples: the Parthenon, the Temple of Athene Nike (Athene Victorious) and the Erectheum. The oldest images of her were the Pallidia, meteors which were supposed to have protective powers. Later on she was represented by wooden statues and thereafter by stone. She always wore an aegis or breastplate and sometimes carried a winged victory in her left hand. Her bird was the owl.

In Lydia there lived a girl called Arachne whose parents were very poor. However, Arachne was a marvellous spinner and embroiderer, so that she brought wealth to her poor parents. She became famous throughout Greece and Ionia and people from far away came to obtain her wares. For some time she and her parents lived happily but unfortunately Arachne's head was turned by all the praise that she received for her work, and one day she boasted that though she was only a poor girl, her work was of a finer quality than that of Athene. Now there was one thing that annoyed the gods and that was conceit, so that when Athene heard what Arachne had said she decided to visit her to see if it was true. She therefore took the form of an old grey-haired woman leaning on a staff and came to the house where Arachne was working. Arachne was surrounded by a circle of admiring people and once again the girl boasted that she could outshine Athene in skill at embroidery and spinning. Athene, in her guise as the old woman, begged her not to claim equality with the gods but to be content to be the best weaver on earth. Arachne got angry and suggested that Athene was afraid to take part in a trial of skill, otherwise she would have appeared to contest Arachne's claim. This was too much for Athene and dropping her staff, she resumed her true shape. All the bystanders fell flat on their faces in awe and respect but Arachne showed no fear and calmly challenged Athene. Without wasting any more time, they began to contest. Each started with an empty loom; Athene's picture represented a famous contest of the gods and in the corners she wove scenes showing what happened to mortals who had opposed the gods in any way, which was meant to be a warning to Arachne. Meanwhile, Arachne worked as though her life depended upon it, which indeed it did. She depicted a beautiful scene of clouds floating in the sky, birds flying and fish swimming in the sea. The moral of her story was that even the gods could make a mistake. When she had finished there was no doubt that Arachne's work was far better than Athene's, who was forced to admit that Arachne had won the contest.

However, when Arachne saw how angry Athene was, she realized that she had made a great mistake in challenging her but it was too late. The goddess seized the beautiful picture that Arachne had made and tore it into pieces. Then she raised her shuttle and struck Arachne three times on the head. Arachne was too proud to accept such treatment. She grasped a rope which lay near and would have hanged herself had she not been stopped by Athene, who said she should live, suspended from a thread and spin for all eternity. In a trice, Arachne's body contracted and became round, her hair fell off and her fingers were changed to many legs. She had become a spider and since then spiders have spun their webs, within houses and without, in gardens and in woods.

In this story, Athene was not shown in a good light but she was usually a fairly reasonable goddess. She helped Prometheus to create mankind, Perseus to fight the Gorgons, assisted Heracles in his labours and welcomed him to Olympus after his death when he was made immortal. She also helped Bellerophon by giving him the golden bridle of Pegasus, the flying horse, and aided Odysseus on his homeward journey.

XVII

The Story of Perseus

This tale comes from Argos. Acrisius was the twin brother of Proetus, the king of Argos. He had a daughter, Danaë, of whom it was prophesied that if she bore a son he would kill his grandfather. To avoid such a happening, Acrisius kept her shut up in a chamber of bronze so no one could come near her. But Zeus, who had already seen her, loved her and visited her in the form of a shower of gold and in due course Danaë bore him a son, Perseus. In fear, Acrisius put Danaë and the child in a wooden chest, which he cast into the sea. Carried by the waves to the island of Seriphus in the Cyclades, they were found by Dictys, who took them to Polydectes, the king of the island, who gave them his protection and there Perseus grew up. Meanwhile, Polydectes had fallen in love with Danaë, who did not return the feeling. To prevent Perseus causing any trouble Polydectes persuaded the young hero to fetch him the head of Medusa the Gorgon, thus hoping to be rid of him for good as anyone who looked at her was turned to stone.

Helped by Athene, Perseus went first to the Graeae, the old grey women who had only a single eye between them. By stealing this and making them temporarily blind, Perseus obtained information from them as to where the Gorgons were. He also acquired from them the cap of invisibility, the winged shoes of swiftness and a wallet in which to carry the head. Armed with a sickle, given him by Hermes, he found the Gorgons, asleep. Flying near Medusa, he was guided by her reflection in his shield, so that he was able to cut off her head before she awoke, put it in the wallet and flee. The other Gorgons tried to give chase but they could not see him as he was wearing the cap of invisibility.

On his way back, he passed near Joppa where he saw Andromeda, daughter of Cepheus, King of Ethiopia, chained to a rock.

64

It appeared that her mother had offended the sea-goddesses by boasting that she was more beautiful than they were, so in revenge, Poseidon had sent a sea monster to devour men and beasts, which could only be propitiated by the sacrifice of the king's daughter. Perseus, who had fallen in love with Andromeda at first sight, offered to kill the monster if he was allowed to marry her. Her parents consented and Perseus turned the monster to stone by showing it the Gorgon's head. Perseus stayed a year with the King of Ethiopia and left behind his first born son as an heir for Cepheus, who had no sons. Then he sailed with Andromeda to Seriphus. There he found his mother suppliant at the altar where Poly-dectes had confined her till she yielded to his will or died of hunger. Perseus rescued her by holding up the Gorgon's head thus turning the king and his men to stone.

Putting the kingship in the hands of Dictys, Perseus and Andromeda went on to Argos only to find that Acrisius had fled to Pelasgiotis in Thessaly, on hearing of his arrival. Whilst in full pursuit of him, Perseus accidentally killed his grandfather when throwing a discus in sport, thus fulfilling the prophecy. Perseus, eventually, retired to Asia where his son, Perses, became the ancestor of the Persians.

XVIII

Eros and Psyche

This story was recounted by Apulius in *The Golden Ass*. Once upon a time there was a king in Greece who had three daughters. The youngest, Psyche, was by far the most beautiful. The two elder daughters soon got married leaving Psyche alone in the palace with her parents. Unfortunately for Psyche, the people of her country regarded her beauty as of special significance and compared her to their local goddess, Aphrodite, to the disadvantage of the goddess. They even ceased to worship at her temple and instead crowded round Psyche whenever she went out, asking for her blessing and offering her their children to lay her hands on. All this was repugnant to Psyche, so she remained at home most of the time. However, this was not to save her from the wrath of Aphrodite, who like all the Greek deities was very jealous. Aphrodite decided to punish her, even though she had done nothing wrong.

About this time, the king consulted the oracle at Delphi, which told him that nothing in his kingdom would go right until he sacrificed his youngest daughter. He was instructed to leave her on a certain rock formation, which was a notable feature of a nearby mountain, where she would be eaten by a monster who lived there, thus distracting its attention from devouring the population of the kingdom. The king does not seem to have questioned this harsh judgement but immediately took Psyche and left her on the mountain. Happily, Psyche was rescued by Zephyrus, the West Wind, who lifted her gently and placed her in a sheltered valley where he set her down in front of a splendid palace. There seemed to be nobody there but when Psyche was hungry, she was miraculously fed by invisible hands. When night fell she went to bed in a comfortable bed, where she was joined by a mysterious presence. Unknown to her, this was Eros, the son of Aphrodite, the most beautiful of the gods, who had been told by his mother to punish Psyche, but captivated by her gentle ways, he had fallen in love with her and had ordered Zephyrus to go to her rescue. Eros warned Psyche that she must never try to look at his face for if she did, disaster would strike and he would disappear never to be seen again.

For some time she lived happily, lacking nothing in the way of comfort but starved of company, she became rather lonely in her splendid palace. Mostly, she missed her sisters and they, in their turn, missed her. Every day they would go up the mountain to the rock from where she had disappeared and mourn her with loud cries and lamentations. One day when the wind was blowing in her direction, Psyche heard their cries and finding her way over the mountain, took them back to the palace where she lived. Her sisters were extremely jealous of her rich clothes, her beautiful furniture and her invisible lover. They envied her good fortune and teased her into thinking that her invisible lover was none other than a horrible monster who was so ugly that he was afraid to show her his face. They begged her to light a lamp so as to discover who she was sleeping with. Finally, unable to bear their taunts any longer and in spite of all the forewarnings of Eros, she lit an oil lamp to find no monster but the handsome Eros lying at her side. Unnerved by the sight, her hand shook and a drop of oil from the lamp fell on his shoulder and burnt him. On waking, Eros accused her of lack of faith and after announcing that she would never see him again, vanished out of sight.

Psyche was devastated. She tried to kill herself, first by jumping off a high place but the wind lifted her up. Then she threw herself into a river which flowed gently to the bank depositing her on the side. This was because Eros, although invisible to her, was continually watching over her. Psyche searched high and low for Eros throughout Greece and finally arrived in Cyprus, the home of Aphrodite, who lived in a splendid palace near Paphos. It was here that Psyche met Aphrodite, who was still determined to punish the girl further and set her a series of difficult tasks.

First Aphrodite asked Psyche to pluck some golden wool from a flock of fierce sheep. Some reeds growing in the field advised her not to approach the sheep until after midday and then not to attempt to pluck the wool but to gather it from the bushes in the field where the sheep had brushed against the branches. This good advice enabled Psyche to collect a whole basket of golden wool for the goddess. Aphrodite, however, was not satisfied and demanded that Psyche fetch a bottle of water from the cold dark stream that fed the waters of the Styx, the river of the Underworld. The stream flowed down a high mountain which was hard to reach. Nevertheless, Psyche climbed the arduous rock face only to find that the stream flowed through a rocky gorge and worse, it was guarded by dragons. While she was peering into the gorge and wondering what to do, the royal eagle of Zeus flew by and taking pity on her asked her what he could do to help. On hearing what task Aphrodite had set her, he took the bottle from her, quickly flew down to the river and filled it, easily out-manoeuvring the dragons. Psyche was thus able to return to Aphrodite with her second task accomplished.

The goddess was not to be placated with this effort either; so this time, she thought up a really difficult task. Psyche was to descend to the Afterworld and ask Persephone for some of her beauty as Aphrodite's had faded somewhat, through having to care for Eros and his burnt shoulder. This task really upset Psyche and she climbed up a high tower intending to cast herself off the top in despair in the hope of reaching the Afterworld by dying. However, the tower was also sorry for her and instructed her what to do to accomplish Aphrodite's wish. She was told that one of the many entries to the Afterworld was nearby and that there was a path leading down to it which she must follow; the entrance was called 'Taenares'. The Tower told her to take some provisions along, not for herself but for those whom she would need to placate on her way. She was advised to take two barley and two honey cakes for Cerberus, the three-headed dog who guarded the entry to the Afterworld, two obels, the smallest Greek coin, to pay Charon, the ferryman, who would ferry her across the Styx and warned that she was in no circumstances to help anyone that she met on the way. The Tower told her that the first person she would see would be a lame man with a lame donkey laden with wood. The man would ask her to help him pick up the sticks that fell from the donkey's load but she was to take no notice and go on her way.

Then when she was crossing the Styx in Charon's boat, she would see a man swimming who would ask her for her help but she was not to reply to his pleas. When she got to the other side of the river, she would see some women weaving who would also ask for help but she was not to assist them either. It seems that all these demands were traps set by Aphrodite to ensnare her and defeat her in her task. Then, when she reached Persephone she would be offered a fine seat to sit upon and food to eat but she was to refuse the seat and sit instead on the ground, where the only food she could eat would be some brown bread. Finally, the Tower told Psyche not to lose the cakes or she would not be able to pass Cerberus and said "If you follow my instructions, you will be able to return to this world. Persephone will give you a box but at all cost do not look inside it, for if you do, it will do you no good."

Everything came to pass exactly as the Tower had foretold, until Psyche, on her way back from the Afterworld, with the box given her by Persephone, was overcome with curiosity as to what it contained. Sitting down by the path she opened the box. She could not see anything but was overcome by a deep sleep and sank senseless to the ground. At this point, she would have died had not Eros, who had been watching over her all the time, flown out of his room in Aphrodite's palace and quickly wiped away the deadly sleep from her eyes and placed it back in the box. He woke her gently and told her how for the second time her curiosity had almost been her undoing and that she must take the box to Aphrodite and await her decision.

Aphrodite was not pleased and set her another task. This time she showed Psyche a large pile of assorted grain: oats, barley, millet, lentils, beans, vetch, and poppy seeds all mixed together. She ordered the girl to separate them, one from another, in the shortest possible time. Psyche thought this to be an impossible task and did not even attempt it but sat staring hopelessly at the pile wondering what to do. A small ant that was passing by felt sorry for her and for all the terrible things she was being asked to do, so it rounded up all its ant friends and relations and set them to work, separating the grains. In no time at all, they had sorted out the grain into separate heaps. Aphrodite, returning home late in the afternoon from one of the many weddings she had to attend and from which she was slightly drunk, was furious to find such a difficult task completed.

Eros, meanwhile, now completely recovered from his burn, flew up to Olympus and laid the matter before Zeus. He fell as a suppliant before the king of the gods and asked for his help in securing Psyche for him. Zeus, thereupon, called a council of the gods and pointed out to them all the trouble that Eros had caused in the past and that if they agreed to him marrying Psyche, it might keep him quiet. Zeus sent for Aphrodite and instructed her to become reconciled to her son and to agree to his marriage to Psyche. Thus it was that Psyche was made immortal by drinking a cup of nectar and her marriage to Eros took place on Mount Olympus, attended by all the gods and goddesses.

The name Psyche, in Greek, represents an aspect of the human soul that can only obtain its ultimate end through pain and tribulation.

XIX

Bellerophon and Pegasus the Winged Horse

Just as Attica had Theseus as its mythical hero, so other places in Greece had legends connected with heroes. Bellerophon was the son of Glaucus, King of Corinth. He was originally called Hipponous but received the name Bellerophon after slaying Bellerus, a Corinthian. To be purified from the murder, he fled to the court of Proëtus, King of Argos, who gave him refuge until his queen, Anteia, fell in love with him. Bellerophon refused her advances but Anteia furious at being spurned, accused him of molesting her and Proëtus, in a rage, sent the hero off to King Iobates of Lycia with a note demanding the king kill him. Iobates, thereupon, sent him to fight the Chimaera, a fire-breathing monster shaped like a lion in front, a dragon behind and a goat (chimaera, hence the name) in the middle.

Now Bellerophon had a winged horse called Pegasus, which had sprung from the blood of Medusa. He had tamed it with a wonderful bridle given to him by Athene in a dream, before he left Corinth. Thus he was able to kill the Chimaera by shooting it with arrows from the air, bestraddled on Pegasus. Iobates, having failed in his mission to have Bellerophon killed by the Chimaera, next sent him to do battle with the Solymi, a fierce local tribe, whom Bellerophon also vanquished. Then he was sent against the Amazons and again he defeated them. Finally, Iobates set an ambush for him, manned by chosen Lycian warriors but Bellerophon succeeded in killing them all. This was all too much for Iobates who realized, at last, that he was dealing with someone exceptional, so he offered Bellerophon the hand of his daughter. Two of their offspring were ill-fated. Their son, Isander, died in the fight against the Solymi, their daughter, Laodameia, was killed by the arrows of Artemis, after she had offended the goddess. And another son,

The winged horse Pegasus.

Hippolochus, was the father of Glaucus, the second in command of the Lycian contingent at Troy.

According to Homer, Bellerophon, now out of favour with the gods, spent his declining years wandering in the Aeolian plain. Later sources say that Bellerophon tried to fly up to Olympus on Pegasus and was punished by the gods for his presumption. He was flung from his horse, from a great height. He escaped death but wandered lame and solitary until he died.

XX

The Faithless King of Troy

Many centuries before the great war between the Trojans and the Greeks, there was a king of Troy called Laomedon. There were at least seven cities called Troy, all built one above the other, and it was in the reign of Laomedon that the great walls were built that defied the Greeks for so long. It is no little wonder these walls were strong because they were built by Poseidon and Apollo.

Poseidon had been temporarily banished by Zeus, who was having one of his jealous spells and suspected Poseidon of intriguing against him, so he imposed a term of service to an earthly king. Thus it was that Poseidon worked for King Laomedon and built the walls of Troy, whilst Apollo lightened the task by playing his lyre. Laomedon had agreed to pay Poseidon generously but rather in the same way that the Norse gods had refused to pay the giant when the walls of Asguard were finished, so Laomedon refused to pay Poseidon, thinking himself secure within his strong walls. Punishment, however, was not long in coming. A large sea-serpent appeared at the behest of Poseidon and started to ravish the coast of Troy eating the inhabitants as it went. All attempts to kill the monster having failed, the Trojans consulted an oracle and were told that they must sacrifice a beautiful maiden once a year. This they did and year after year the Trojans paid this awful tribute to the sea monster, until the lot fell upon the Princess Hesione, the only daughter of King Laomedon.

King Laomedon was overwhelmed with grief, as he was devoted to his only daughter and was powerless to protect her. So he issued a proclamation promising her hand to any hero who could destroy the monster. On hearing the proclamation by the king's herald, Heracles went immediately to Troy. Meanwhile, the fateful day had arrived when the maiden was to be taken down to the sea-shore and chained to the rock from which the monster would take her. The priests had already left and the king was just turning away so as not to see the monster eating his child when Heracles appeared. Pausing momentarily to cheer up the king, he sped down to the sea-shore where the monster was rearing from the sea, roaring dreadfully as it advanced to seize its prey. Heracles smote its head with his powerful club and after several blows left it lying lifeless at the feet of Hesione.

But once again Laomedon broke his word and failed to hand over the girl to the hero. Heracles was furious and went to Greece returning with a group of heroes and six galleys. He attacked the city and on reaching the palace, he killed both the king and queen. Hesione was carried off to Greece and married Telamon, a friend and companion of Heracles.

XXI

The Halcyon Days

Once, somewhere in mainland Greece or the Greek islands, there lived a king and queen called Ceyx and Alcyone. Alcyone was a Pleiade, the daughter of Atlas and Pleïone. The king and queen were devoted to one another and lived happily together for many years, until Ceyx had to go on a long journey to consult an oracle. This meant a sea voyage and Alcyone did not want him to go. However, he felt he must and after having put it off as long as possible, he set sail. Alcyone was there to see him off, her heart full of foreboding for the dangers he would undergo. She waved for as long as she could see him, then returned to the palace to pray for a safe voyage.

At first all went well. The wind was from the right direction and the ship made good progress, but on the fifth day, towards the evening, dark clouds began to gather and a storm arose. For a time the ship ran before the gale, then there was thunder and lightning and the wind blew so fiercely that the sailors could not hear the orders shouted by Ceyx. Soon the mast and sail went overboard and the vessel drifted helplessly, at the mercy of the waves. The broken mast had stove in the side and the water poured in, so that eventually the vessel sank. Ceyx grasped a spar and for a while floated on the surface of the sea but the waves were very high and a cross-current tore him off the spar. He was only able to murmur the name Alcyone, before he, like his crew, was drowned in the Aegean Sea.

Meanwhile, Alcyone had gone every day to pray at the temple of Hera, protectress of the hearth and home, for the safe return of her husband. After a while, Hera could no longer bear the sound of her prayers calling for the safe return of a man who was already dead, so she sent for Iris, the messenger of the gods (Iris was a winged deity, who was said to have originally been the personification of the rainbow linking heaven and earth with its multicoloured rays). Thereupon, Hera sent Iris to the dark cavern of Somnus, God of Sleep. The cavern was always wrapped in darkness, deep night always dwelt there and the silence was complete. Outside near the threshold, grew those plants that like the poppy, promoted sleep, whilst in the centre of the cavern, on a black couch, lay Somnus, wrapped in slumber surrounded by floating shadowy figures of dreams and visions.

When beautiful Iris, with her incandescent wings, entered the cavern she filled the whole place with bright light and awakened by this, Somnus raised his weary head. Iris spoke to him and addressed him thus, 'O Somnus, gentlest of gods, brother of Death, who brings peace and rest to weary mankind, I come to you from Hera who begs you to send a vision to Alcyone telling her of Ceyx's shipwreck'. After having spoken these words, the gentle Iris sped out of the cave into the bright sunlight beyond.

Somnus looked among his visions and chose a gentle one and bade him take the form of Ceyx and go and visit Alcyone in the palace that very night. With swift and silent wings he soared through the night until he arrived at the palace and stood at the bedside of Alcyone. He looked just like her husband but not as she had last seen him but wet and dripping, his hands encrusted with barnacles and with seaweed in his wet hair. Alcyone awoke from the dream but there was no one there. She was so disturbed by the dream that she rose and dressed and went down to the sea-shore, where she had bidden her husband farewell. She stood there for a long time, watching the light of dawn grow stronger, until she saw a white object being washed ashore by the waves. It became clear that it was the body of her husband, just as she had seen it in her dream. This was too much for Alcyone, who felt that she could not live without Ceyx and climbed a neighbouring cliff and flung herself off to drown herself.

But she was not drowned. Hera, who pitied her, turned her and Ceyx into halcyon birds, or kingfishers, which live forever on the surface of the sea. Sailors say that even in the stormiest weather, there are seven calm days in every year when the water is smooth and only gentle winds blow. These are known as the halcyon days because it is only then that the halcyon birds can be seen floating on the water.

76

XXII

Daedalus and the First Flight

Once, in Ancient Athens, there lived a very clever craftsman called Daedalus, who made beautiful statues. Not only did he work in stone but he also made wonderful carvings in wood. He was said to have invented the saw and the axe. Now Daedalus had a nephew called Perdix, a clever lad, who wished to learn his uncle's trade. He became apprenticed to Daedalus and, before long, showed signs of becoming an even better craftsman than his uncle. Athenians soon sang his praises and people began to say that he would turn out to be more famous than Daedalus. This annoyed Daedalus so much that he became jealous, and one day he took Perdix for a walk along the cliffs, near Sunion, and pushed him off a ledge hoping to kill him. However, Athene had observed what was happening and turned the young man into a partridge as he fell towards the waves. The bird has born his Greek name ever since.

It was not long before the people of Athens started asking what had become of Perdix and all sorts of rumours went round the city. Daedalus was afraid the Athenians would harm him if they knew the truth, so he hurriedly left for Crete, taking his young son, Icarus, with him. In Crete he went to the court of King Minos at Knossos, where he was greeted kindly and was given work by the king. The most remarkable thing that he made for King Minos was the construction of the Labyrinth, a skilful maze, with endless passages leading to a room in the middle where the Minotaur was kept. The Minotaur was a fearful monster, half man and half bull, which the king wished to keep shut up in a safe place. It was the offspring of a beautiful bull, sent to Minos by Poseidon, which Minos had failed to sacrifice as he should have done.

It was Daedalus who helped Ariadne when she gave Theseus the thread to find his way out of the Labyrinth and for that transgression, King Minos had Daedalus and Icarus locked up in the Labyrinth. In order to escape, Daedalus fashioned a pair or wings for himself and a pair for his son, made of feathers and attached by wax. After warning Icarus to stay close beside him and telling him neither to fly too high nor too low, they sped away. Icarus, enchanted by the power of flight, soared too near the sun; the wax melted and Icarus plummeted into the sea and drowned. Daedalus buried his son on a nearby island, now known as Icaria, and the sea thereabouts as the Icarian Sea. After this tragedy, Daedalus flew on to Sicily, where he was received by King Cocalus. It was here that he gained great fame, erecting many fine buildings.

XXIII

Echo and Narcissus

Echo was a nymph who lived in the woods and danced and sang with other nymphs. She was very talkative, fond of telling stories and always liked to have the last word in any argument. Hera was quite fond of her and used to come down to earth to listen to her stories until she discovered that Echo was telling these tales at the request of Zeus in order to keep her occupied so as to have more time to himself. Hera was really annoyed when she found out that she had been duped and she decided to punish Echo. Her punishment took a strange form. She deprived Echo of the power of speech but allowed her to mimic the last word that people uttered. This is particularly characteristic of speech in mountainous areas and we call the sound 'an echo' after the nymph.

Now it so happened that living in the same part of the woods was a handsome youth called Narcissus, the son of Cephissus and his wife Liriope. When he was born his mother consulted a wise man to foretell Narcissus's future, to see if her son would survive until manhood. The seer replied "He will if he never recognizes himself". No one could explain this prediction to her. Now although Narcissus had many good qualities, he did not have many friends. One day he was out hunting, a sport of which he was inordinately fond, when he came to the part of the oak forest where Echo lived. The moment Echo caught sight of Narcissus, she fell in love with him and followed him through the forest, seeking for some means of communication with him. They went on for some time until Narcissus realized that he had lost his way and he called out hoping someone was within earshot. "Is anyone here?" Echo who had hidden behind a tree replied, "Here". The youth was very surprised at this as he had imagined that he was alone. He looked all over the place but could see no one, so he called out "Come" and Echo immediately replied "Come". This confused Narcissus because every time he spoke, his last word was repeated. Echo was frightened lest he become angry, so she remained hidden. Finally, he called "Let us come together here" and Echo taking this as an invitation, rushed forward and flung her arms round him. Narcissus, who did not like being touched, was most upset and roughly flung her away and journeyed deeper into the woods. Poor Echo, his unkind words and behaviour had deeply wounded her. She hid in the woods refusing all sustenance and eventually pined away and died. Only her voice remained.

Narcissus continued to hunt frequently and one day, thirsty after being out since dawn, found a little clear spring in the woods and flung himself down to take a drink. Suddenly he paused, for reflected in the water was the most beautiful face that he had ever seen. He looked in wonder and as he looked it seemed to grow ever more beautiful. You must remember, that in those days mirrors were a rarity and far beyond the means of a simple hunter, so that Narcissus would have no idea of what he looked like. He spoke to the face in the water but though its lips moved it made no reply. Narcissus was enchanted; he had fallen in love with his own image. He tried to approach nearer but when he touched the water, the image vanished. He remained by the stream, losing all desire for food and gradually pined away and died. The seer's words had come true. His final words were addressed to his reflection in the stream, "O youth beloved in vain, farewell". Echo's spirit which had stayed near at hand hoping to be able to help him, replied "Farewell".

The nymphs of the river and the woods who had known him, prepared a funeral pyre for him, but when they went to recover his body from beside the stream, it had vanished. Instead, a beautiful flower was growing in its place, with a lovely golden centre and white petals, nodding at its reflection in the stream. To this day, the flower is called after the youth, Narcissus, and is found by quiet streams and pools, gazing forever at itself in the water.

XXIV

Pygmalion and Galatea

In the city of Amanthus, on the south coast of Cyprus, lived a sculptor called Pygmalion. His work was famous throughout the island and he was commissioned to carve all the statues of the gods and goddesses for the temples. He was an excellent sculptor and lived only for his work, but he was very lonely. One day, an especially fine piece of marble was delivered to his workshop; on seeing the stone he felt inspired, but before starting work, he prayed to Aphrodite, the patron goddess of the island, that he might make something very special. His mind was obsessed with the vision of a beautiful woman, more lovely than any woman he had actually seen. As he worked on the life-size figure, he found he was unable to concentrate on anything else. He even abandoned hunting of which he was especially fond. Gradually the figure neared completion. Pygmalion had portrayed a woman standing with one arm extended and in her outstretched hand a rose; it looked exactly as if the statue was about to step forward.

By this time, Pygmalion had fallen deeply in love with the figure that he had made and was unwilling that anyone else should see it. He, therefore, took the statue from his workshop to his bedroom and placed it in a niche in the wall. He even dressed it in fine garments and jewels, and scattered flowers from his garden at its feet, filling the room with a delightful scent.

Not long afterwards, Pygmalion was awoken one morning by the sound of a religious procession to Aphrodite passing the house. They were carrying one of the statues he had made of her, round the town to the temple, all freshly garlanded, as it was her feast day. The procession was formed by men and maidens singing and dancing in honour of the goddess. Pygmalion was normally far too busy to join in, but today he decided to do so and picking some leaves to make a wreath, he hurried after the procession to join in. When it reached the temple, the goddess was returned to her customary place, which had been swept clean and strewn with sweet blooms while she had been away. Soon after the statue had been replaced, everyone withdrew, save for the few who wished to make some special petition. Pygmalion was one of those. He obtained some incense and placed it upon the altar, whereupon flames shot skywards in recognition of the offering. While the incense smouldered, Pygmalion prayed to the goddess that as a great favour, his statue should be given life.

Pygmalion returned home, feeling that perhaps he had been presumptious to ask for such a favour. When he went to his room, he found the niche empty and thought the statue had been stolen, but then he heard his name being called softly and when he turned he saw a figure standing by the window. When he had left, the figure had been of stone and now on his return, it had become a living, breathing human being, who said to him 'Pygmalion, Aphrodite has heard your prayer and has given me life so that I can become your wife." Pygmalion could hardly believe what he heard and asked her how it had come about. She responded that she remembered standing in the niche and seeing the goddess standing in front of her. The goddess told her to come down from the niche and then she dressed her in the saffron robe that she herself was wearing. Aphrodite had kissed her and said that she would love Pygmalion as much as he loved her, and then gave her the name Galatea, after one of the sea nymphs. She prophesied that Pygmalion and Galatea would live happily ever after. Pygmalion was astounded but everything turned out as Aphrodite had foretold. Galatea made him a good and loving wife and they lived together happily for many years until they died in the fullness of time.

XXV

Philemon and Baucis

The gods, as you know, can change their shapes at will and were always anxious to see how things were going on, on earth. Once they heard bad accounts of a town in Greece, so Zeus and Hermes decided to go and see for themselves, how things were. When they got to the town, instead of being welcomed, they were followed through the streets by crowds of children jeering at them and throwing stones. They tried various houses to see if they could obtain shelter for the night. At the first house, no one answered their knocking, although there were lights on and they could hear voices. At the second house they tried, they were having a party and someone opened an upper window and told them to go away. And so it was with house after house, either no answer at all or a very dusty one. After they had visited all the houses in the town, they felt tired, cold and hungry.

On the outskirts of the town, stood a poor little hut with the roof in need of repair, and here the gods stopped. It was owned by an old couple, Philemon and his wife Baucis, who asked them in and explained that they were very poor but that if the travellers would like to share their simple fare, they were very welcome. The fire was piled high with logs and Zeus and Hermes were offered some milk to drink. The gods enjoyed it and asked for more, which worried Baucis as she knew that nearly all the milk had been drunk. However, when she looked in the pitcher, she saw that it was full and it was to remain full all evening, no matter how often the glasses were refilled. There was only bread to eat and some honey from their beehive, with a few grapes from the vine growing over the porch. Baucis was surprised to find that the honey was more golden and the grapes far sweeter than she had ever remembered before. After a time, the visitors indicated that they would like to rest, so Philemon and Baucis showed them into their bedroom to the only bed the cottage had, while they went to sleep on the floor by the fire.

The old couple rose early in the morning, as their visitors had eaten everything in the house and the only thing left to give them was their goose. As they were trying to catch it, their visitors appeared in the doorway and asked them to go with them to the top of a nearby hill. When they reached the top, Zeus turned to them and said, "You have been entertaining the gods unaware, fear not, but look and see where your town was." They looked and saw that where the town had been, there was now a sparkling lake, and where their cottage had been, was a beautiful marble temple. The wicked people who had refused the gods hospitality, had all been destroyed. Zeus then offered them anything they would like. Philemon and Baucis thought for a moment and then said, "Please allow us to become guardians of your beautiful temple for as long as we live and as we do not want to live without one another, let us die together." Their wish was granted and for many years they remained as guardians of the temple to Zeus. They welcomed all strangers and were just as good and hospitable after their good fortune, as they had been before.

Finally, they grew very old and life no longer seemed so good to them. One evening as they were standing in front of the temple thinking what a happy time they had had there, they vanished to be replaced by two majestic trees whose upper branches were intertwined. So Philemon and Baucis had their wish and lived on together in the trees they had become. Strangers, visiting the place and hearing the story, used to hang garlands in the trees and sit beneath their shade listening to the wind, and as long as the temple stood, they were never forgotten.

XXVI

The House of Cadmus

Cadmus and Europa were two of the children of King Agenor of Tyre. One day, Zeus abducted Europa, and Agenor sent his sons to look for her, threatening them with banishment if they did not find her. Cadmus, accompanied by his mother Telephassa, got as far as Thrace, where Telephassa died, worn out with sorrow. After burying her, Cadmus consulted the oracle at Delphi to ask Apollo's advice on what to do next because although his brothers had given up the search for Europa, Cadmus was more persistent. The oracle instructed him to go to a desert place where he would find a cow, which he was to follow until she finally lay down and there he was to build a city and name it after himself, Cadmeia. All this Cadmus did and eventually Cadmeia became the citadel of the city of Thebes, in the state of Boeotia, which means the land of the cow.

Before founding the city, Cadmus felt he should make a sacrifice to the gods by offering them the cow; so he sent his men to find water with which to purify the offering. Nearby they found a spring, guarded by a fierce dragon, which was really a son of Ares. The dragon killed several of Cadmus's men when they tried to take some of the water and after a struggle, Cadmus managed to kill the dragon. Athene appeared and told him to plough the adjacent land and sow it with the dragon's teeth. Immediately, armed men sprang from the earth, attacked one another and fought until only five were left. These five men were known as the Sparti or Sown-men, and were to become the future leaders of Thebes.

For killing the dragon, Cadmus had to become a servant of Ares for seven years, to work off his blood guilt. At the end of the seven years, Ares was said to have been appeased and gave Cadmus his daughter Harmonia to wed. All the deities came to the wedding and Cadmus gave his bride a wonderful robe, woven by the Charities (the Graces in Latin), as well as a marvellous necklace made by Hephaestus. These gifts turned out to be unlucky and later caused a great deal of trouble. For some time, they lived happily at Thebes where Cadmus is reputed to have introduced the alphabet to Greece. A story based partly on fact as the Greek alphabet is founded upon the Phoenician and Cadmus was a Phoenician. Cadmus and Harmonia had four daughters, Ino, Semele, Autonoë and Agave and it was the son of Agave, Pentheus, who is said to have succeeded Cadmus on the throne of Thebes.

Things had not been going well for Cadmus, so he and Harmonia left Thebes and went to Illyria, where he became king and ruled over the Illyrians for some time. Whilst there, they had a son called Illyrius and for a long time they lived happily but misfortune still pursued Cadmus and his descendants, who also suffered terrible misfortune. Cadmus finally traced the cause of all his troubles back to the fact that he had killed the dragon, the son of Ares and in spite of doing penance, Ares had never really forgiven him for killing his son. Cadmus then prayed to the gods that if this indeed were the cause of his misfortunes, the gods should turn himself and his wife into serpents. The words had hardly crossed his lips before first he and then Harmonia were changed into snakes. However, ill luck continued to strike Thebes. Finally the seer, Teresias, discovered that the only way to expiate the blood guilt of the city for the death of the son of Ares was by sacrificing the youngest of the Sparti. This happened to be Menoeceus, the youngest son of Creon of Thebes, who willingly undertook to give his life to save Thebes and stabbing himself on the walls of the city, he fell into the dragon's old lair and died.

In Thebes, Cadmus and Harmonia were worshipped as almost godlike. They were revered as the inventors of agriculture, the authors of irrigation and the teachers of the art of writing.

XXVII

Ino Daughter of Cadmus

Ino, the daughter of Cadmus, married King Athamas of Thebes by whom she had two sons, Learchus and Melicertes. However, Ino was Athamas's second wife and she was jealous of her stepchildren, a boy Phrixus and a girl Helle, whom she would have liked to have killed. She devised a devilish plan in order to accomplish this. She persuaded the women of Boeotia to roast the seed corn so that it would not sprout and when Athamas enquired of the Delphic oracle the reason why, Ino bribed the messengers to tell Athamas that the god required the sacrifice of Phrixus and Helle to Zeus. Zeus, fortunately, saved the children by sending a golden ram on which they flew east to Colchis. Phrixus was the only one to survive the journey as Helle fell off and drowned in the straits, known thereafter as the Hellespont in her memory.

Hera, Queen of the Gods, was angry with Ino because Ino had persuaded Athamas to take in her nephew Dionysus and bring him up with their sons, after the death of her sister Semele. The goddess planned to make Ino mad but to do so she needed the help of the Furies, who were the children of Night and lived in Hades. Hera discovered a route to the Underworld, shaded by yew trees, that descended steeply into the earth where she found the Furies guarding the greatest sinners like Tityus the giant, son of Gaea, Tantalus, a son of Zeus and Sisyphus, the most cunning of mortals, legendary founder of Corinth and brother of Athamas. When Hera arrived, the Furies were busy combing back the snakes that formed their hair. When they saw Hera they recognized her and rose to greet her. Hera explained to them that she wanted to make Ino and Athamas insane and wanted their help. The Fury Tisiphone agreed to help her, and Hera, her task accomplished, returned to Olympus, where as she entered the sacred portals, she was purified by Iris, the messenger of the gods.

Tisiphone, clothed in a blood-stained garment and with a couple of snakes coiled round her waist and many more in her hair, went to the palace of Athamas accompanied by Grief, Terror and Madness. She took her stand in the doorway of the palace and even the very door posts turned pale with fright. The sun fled from the sky and Ino and Athamas were overcome with terror and tried to flee. However, Tisiphone blocked their way and stretching out her arms which were covered with writhing vipers, shook her head so that hissing snakes fell in coils over her shoulders. She flung two of the snakes at Ino and Athamas and they crawled all over the terrified humans instilling poison into their minds. Whirling her flaming torch, the Fury descended into the Underworld, her task completed.

Athamas, now raving mad, called out that he had just seen a lioness and her two cubs in the palace. Thinking his wife was the lioness, he snatched from her arms one of their two sons and dashed out his brains on the floor. Ino, terrified and also mad, took Melicertes the other boy and fled from the palace to a steep cliff above the sea and flung herself and the child over the edge, into the foaming water below. The Sea God was sorry for her and transformed her into the White Goddess of the spray called Leucothea. He also took pity on Melicertes and transformed him into the young sea god, Palaemon, whose duty it is to guard sailors during storms.

XXVIII

Dionysus

Dionysus was believed to be a foreign god from Thessaly or Phrygia. His father was Zeus and his mother, Zemelo, the Phrygian Earth Goddess. In Greek mythology, Zemelo became Semele, the daughter of Cadmus, much loved by Zeus. Their love affair made Hera very jealous and she plotted Semele's destruction. In the guise of an old woman, she suggested Semele should test the love of Zeus by asking him to appear before her in his divine form, knowing that as a mortal, Semele would be consumed by the lightning he carried within him. Zeus who had agreed never to deny her anything she asked, could not refuse and Semele was duly consumed by his divine fire. Zeus snatched their unborn child from Semele's ashes and thrust him into his thigh for protection, from where, in due course, Dionysus was born. He was brought up by Ino, a sister of Semele, until she died and then he was cared for by the Nymphs of Nysa, on a mountain. He was surrounded by Satyrs and with his head crowned in ivy and laurel, the young god wandered on the mountain slopes.

When Dionysus grew up he discovered the vine and he is said to have invented the art of making wine. Hera is believed to have sent him mad but the oracle of Dodona cured him. He travelled extensively, introducing wine to the world and had many adventures. From Thrace he went to Boeotia and thence to Attica, where he was made welcome by the king, Icarius, who unwisely gave his shepherds wine to drink. They got very drunk and then thought the king was trying to poison them, so they murdered him. His daughter, Erigone, with her dog, Maera, went to look for him and when she found him dead, was so distressed, she killed herself. The gods changed them into constellations, the Waggoner, Virgo and the Lesser Dog Star.

Dionysus proceeded with his travels to Phrygia where he was initiated into the mysteries of Cybele, to Syria where he planted the vine, Egypt and Libya. He is also credited with a civilizing mission to India. When in Laconia, he fell in love with the youngest daughter of King Dion. Her sisters objected, so Dionysus made them lose their minds and turned the youngest into a walnut tree.

One of the best stories about Dionysus is told in the Homeric Hymn no. VII. Dionysus was sitting on a headland one day, wearing a purple cloak, when a ship of Tyrrhenian pirates passed by. They thought he would make a good captive, so fell upon him and bound him with heavy cord, but in vain. The knots came undone and the bonds fell off, so the helmsman suggested they should release him. However, the pirates certain they would get a good ransom for him, kept him on board. Wine started to flow from the mast and a vine grew up over the sails and whilst they were arguing what to do, Dionysus turned into a fierce lion and grasped the master. The sailors leapt overboard and were immediately changed into dolphins; only the helmsman was spared. This story was used to explain why dolphins are so friendly to man.

In Naxos, Dionysus met Ariadne, daughter of King Minos of Crete. She had been deserted by Theseus after their flight from Crete and the killing of the Minotaur. Dionysus consoled Ariadne and married her and they had three sons. Festivals to celebrate their marriage were held in Naxos and Ariadne's tomb was supposed to be in that island.

Dionysus's extensive travels ultimately changed him and on his return to Greece he was no longer the rustic god of mountains and shepherds but a rather effeminate youth responsible for introducing orgiastic rites from Phrygia. He was followed by revellers, some divine, some human, nymphs, satyrs and Bacchantes (female followers who went into the woods at full moon and became filled with mysterious ecstasy). As a result, he was received with some hostility. Thrace turned against him and the king, Lycurgus, imprisoned some of his followers. Dionysus responded by making him mad, which caused him to kill his own son. Thrace became a wilderness and did not recover until the king was sacrificed.

After a time, Dionysus returned to Thebes, his mother's city, whose king was Pentheus, son of Echion, one of the five Sparti who had sprung from the dragon's teeth before the foundation of

Dionysus.

Thebes. Pentheus's mother, Agave, was another of the daughters of Cadmus. King Pentheus objected to the new rites introduced by Dionysus and considered the excessive drinking to be subversive. He decided to spy on the Bacchantes and disguising himself as a woman, climbed a high pine tree from where he could overlook their activities. Agave, who was taking part in the rites, saw him and mistaking him for a wild beast, she and her friends tore him limb from limb. Then placing his head on a pole, they returned in triumph to Thebes. Only when they reached the city did Agave realize she was carrying the head of her son and that she was the one who had killed him. This terrible fate was retribution for the slaying of the dragon, son of Ares, by Cadmus. When Agave returned to her senses, she fled from Thebes to Illyria, where she married the king, Lycotherses. However, the gods had not finished with her and she was induced to murder her husband so that Cadmus, her father, should have the throne.

Meanwhile, Dionysus rescued his mother, Semele, from Hades in exchange for something he was very attached to: the myrtle. It is said that he gave the god of the Underworld the myrtle, which is the plant worn by initiates into the mysteries of his cult, as a crown of leaves upon their heads. He was worshipped all over Greece but it varied considerably from place to place. One of his oldest festivals was the Agrionia, held in Boeotia, where a young boy was sacrificed. Most unusually, there were human sacrifices elsewhere in Greece and in the Greek Islands, notably in Chios and Lesbos. Attica celebrated three main feasts in his honour, in December, February and March. The latter, the Great Dionysia, was the most important. It was during these festivals that dramatic performances took place and the worship of Dionysus was always closely associated with the theatre. Many Hellenistic theatres were decorated with scenes from his life and travels.

XXIX

Artemis and Actaeon

Artemis was very fond of hunting and used to spend all day in the forest with her maidens. As a result, they used to get very hot and tired, especially in the warm Greek summer. In order to get cool, they would bathe in one of the pools, or in the springs that gushed out of the mountainside. No one was supposed to look at them while they did this and it was well-known that Artemis hated to be watched and spied upon.

One day a young hunter called Actaeon, grandson of Cadmus, was hunting in the forest with his deer hounds and in the heat of summer he became tired and thirsty. He heard the sound of running water and overjoyed that he and his hounds could have a drink, Actaeon parted the bushes. Thereupon he discovered Artemis and her maidens who had been bathing, lying about on the grass at the water's edge. Artemis was just going for another bathe and was not at all pleased to see the young man. She countered 'Impious mortal, how dare you come into my sacred places. This will be the last thing that you do. You will never be allowed to go home and say that you have seen Artemis and her maidens bathing'. So saying, she sprinkled water in his face and Actaeon, who had stood there bewildered by the goings on, found himself transformed into a deer.

He tried to speak but found he could not utter a word. He looked round in terror and heard, in the distance, the baying of his hounds coming to join him. Quickly he turned to flee but it was already too late as the dogs had caught his scent. Though he could run very fast, the forest was not easy to get through, especially with antlers on his head and he kept being dragged back, unable to go where he wished. It was not long before, worn out with the struggle of a body that he was not used to, he sank to the ground exhausted, and was torn to pieces by his own hounds, who had failed to recognize him.

XXX

The Story of Oedipus

The dynasty which was to rule Thebes after the House of Cadmus was that of Labdakidai. Labdacus, the first king, had a son Laius, who was a minor when his father died. Lycus, a Sparti, seized the throne banishing Laius, who took refuge with Pelops, the son of Tantalus. Pelops was a good friend to Laius but betrayed him by kidnapping Pelops's son Chrysippus, a handsome youth. This sin against Pelops was the root of the curse which brought the line of Laius to an end within two generations.

After Lycus and his sons had died, Laius returned to the throne of Thebes, bringing the curse with him. He married Iocaste, daughter of Menoeceus, and was warned by the Delphic Oracle that if they had a son, the son would kill him. In due course, Iocaste gave birth to a son and Laius drove a stake through the child's feet and gave instructions that he should be left to die of exposure on the slopes of Mount Cithaeron, where the shepherds of Thebes and Corinth grazed their flocks. A shepherd of King Polybus of Corinth found the boy and took him to Queen Merope, the wife of Polybus; she reared him as her own, calling him Oedipus, meaning 'swollen feet', as his feet were deformed as a result of the stake. On reaching manhood, Oedipus went to Delphi to ask Apollo who his real parents were, because a youth had tormented him and suggested he was illegitimate. The oracle, however, foretold a terrible fate for him saying he would kill his father and marry his mother. As he knew no other parents save Polybus and Merope, he vowed never to return to Corinth in case the prediction should come true. One day, on the road between Phocis and Boeotia, he met King Laius, whose attendants rudely ordered him off the path so that the king's chariot might pass. Oedipus argued with them until words became blows and during the ensuing fight he killed King Laius, not realizing that he was his real father.

Oedipus arrived in Thebes to find it in a state of turmoil. The king was missing and the inhabitants were being continuously tormented by a monster, the Sphinx (strangler) described as having a woman's face, the body of a lion with wings, who asked a riddle that no one could answer and killed those who failed to do so. Creon, the queen's brother, who was acting as regent, now offered the crown of Thebes to any hero who could answer the riddle, as well as the hand in marriage of the queen. Oedipus undertook the challenge and was accordingly asked the riddle. 'There is on earth a two-footed creature and a four-footed creature with the same name and also a three-footed creature. For it changes its form alone of those that move on the earth, or through the air or in the sea. But when it walks supported by most feet, then is the swiftness of its limbs the weakest". Oedipus gave answer, "You have spoken of man, who when he goes upon the ground is at first four-footed from his mother's womb, but in old age, he leans upon a staff as a third foot". On having answered the riddle correctly, sources vary as to the fate of the Sphinx, who mortified at her riddle being solved, either threw herself down from the rock on which she lived and committed suicide, or was killed by Oedipus.

Oedipus and the Sphinx.

Having saved Thebes from the Sphinx, Oedipus married Iocaste, and as far as is known they lived together for many years quite happily before they found out about their true relationship. They had by this time four children, two sons, Eteocles and Polyneices, and two daughters, Antigone and Ismene. Oedipus, still determined to find out about the truth of his birth, again consulted the Delphic Oracle. He also wanted to find out the cause of a plague that had broken out in Thebes, which indicated that the gods were displeased with the city or with those who administered it. The oracle announced that the plague could not be stopped until the murder of Laius had been avenged. According to Sophocles, after the death of King Polybus of Corinth, a messenger was sent to Thebes to ask Oedipus to become King of Corinth but Oedipus refused, declaring that he dare not return for fear of marrying his mother. The messenger appears to have been the shepherd who had rescued him from the mountainside, and it was from him that Oedipus learnt the truth. In despair, realizing that he had killed his father and married his mother, he blinded himself, whereupon Iocaste committee suicide.

Accounts vary as to what happened next. One version claims that Creon banished Oedipus and that he wandered from place to place attended by his daughter Antigone, finally dying at Colonus in Attica. Another account of his fate relates that he remained imprisoned in his palace until his sons reached manhood. Meanwhile the state was ruled by Creon, but when Oedipus's sons grew up, they did not show the proper respect for their father that he had expected, so he cursed them. The curse was to be fulfilled in that neither of them would agree as to who was to have the kingship.

This legend with its tragedy greatly appealed to the ancient Greeks and was the subject of the tragedies of Aeschylus and Sophocles in particular. There is evidence that the legend, at least, is Mycenaean in date, as Homer speaks of Odysseus wandering in Hades and meeting Iocaste, who had committed suicide when she found she had married her son. Further evidence comes from two Mycenaean gem-stones from Thisbe in Boeotia, the first showing a young man in front of a sphinx; this could represent Oedipus. The second gem-stone shows the same young man aiming an arrow at a man in a chariot, who could be Laius.

XXXI

The Seven against Thebes

The following story is one of the Theban legends.

Adrastus, the King of Argos, had two daughters, Deïpyle and Argeia. He had been told by an oracle that one of his daughters would marry a boar and the other a lion. One day, there arrived at his court two young men who had been banished from their kingdoms, Polyneices of Thebes sporting a lion skin over his shoulder and Tydeus of Calydon who wore a boar skin. Thus it was that Adrastus recognized them as the predicted bridegrooms and married Deïpyle to Tydeus and Argeia to Polyneices, giving Argeia the "fatal necklace" of Hephaestus, though how he obtained it, is uncertain.

Polyneices was a son of Oedipus, King of Thebes and, after Oedipus died, his two sons Eteoclus and Polyneices could not agree who was to have the kingdom. Finally, they decided to rule on alternate years but at the end of the first year, Eteoclus refused to give up the throne and Polyneices was banished and took refuge in Argos.

Adrastus was determined to restore his sons-in-law to their kingdoms and gathered a large army for a war with Thebes commanded by himself, Polyneices and Tydeus, Capaneus and Hippomedon, who were Argives, Parthenopaeüs and the reluctant Amphiaraüs. They became known as the Seven against Thebes. Amphiaraüs, who could foresee the future, knew that the expedition would be a failure and that he himself would die. He also foresaw that Polyneices would enlist his wife Eriphyle, sister of Adrastus, to persuade him to go, so he forebade her to accept any gifts from Polyneices. However, Polyneices managed to bribe her with the "fatal necklace" and Amphiaraüs, who was bound by oath to always agree with his wife's behests, was obliged to go to war, once she had decided that he should. Before he went, he constrained his son Alcmaeon to avenge his death upon his mother, and told him that he, in turn, would march against Thebes and would succeed where the Seven would fail.

The expedition began its march without any problems until it reached Nemea. Here their troubles began. An event took place which led to the founding of the Nemean games, an incident which serves to date the war of the Seven against Thebes to a period after the Argonauts but before the Trojan War. The army eventually reached Thebes, where on arrival each of its seven gates was assigned to one of the seven commanders. The names of the gates and their assailants has varied according to the authority, thus Aeschylus's list is not the same as that given by Euripedes and so on. However, the assault resulted in a complete defeat for the army of Argos. Capaneus was struck by Zeus for boasting on reaching the top of the walls; Tydeus was mortally wounded as he had behaved with so little courage that Athene refused to help him, and Amphiaraüs, who had foreseen the disaster, fled in his chariot and was swallowed up by the earth. The spot where he disappeared became renowned afterwards for its oracles.

Having held the gates against the Seven, the Theban army descended into the plain before their city where there was bitter fighting. Finally, Eteoclus suggested that the battle should be settled by a single-handed contest between him and his brother Polyneices. After a fierce struggle, they both mortally wounded one another, so no one won.

The only leader to escape was Adrastus, and he only got away because of the speed of his horse Arion. Creon, the uncle of Eteoclus and Polyneices and a former regent, now became king but it was a much depleted Thebes that he ruled over, having lost half his fighting men. The Thebans buried their dead with honour but on Creon's orders, left the bodies of their opponents to rot where they had fallen. His act in forbidding burial went against all accepted Greek practice, as unless the proper rites were carried out, the dead were thought to wander forever at the gates of Hades. Not only did Creon order the bodies to be left, he also forbade anyone, on pain of death, to remove them. This was more than Antigone, the sister of Polyneices, could bear and she crept out at night, found her brother's body and covered it with earth. Unfortunately she was seen, and the following night when she returned to observe the proper rituals over it, she was apprehended and taken before Creon. Despite being his niece and a member of the royal family, he was not prepared to save her and had her bricked up in a tomb where she hanged herself. (There are several versions of what happened). Antigone had been engaged to Creon's son Haemon, but on hearing her fate he tried to rescue her but when he found her dead, he killed himself in remorse over her body. His mother, Eurydice, thereupon committed suicide when she heard of her son's death but Creon lived on for many years until dethroned and killed by Lycus the Sparti.

The war of the Seven against Thebes had several important results. The sons of the fallen leaders mounted a second attack on Thebes and this time they were successful. Adrastus, now an old man, once again led the army but died of grief at Megara, on the way home, as his son had been killed in the campaign.

THE NEMEAN GAMES

Hypsipyle was the nurse of Opheltes, the son of King Lycurgus of Nemea. She came originally from the island of Lemnos where she had been Jason's mistress when the Argonauts ravished all the women of Lemnos. Earlier on, she had spared her father when the Lemnian women murdered all the men on the island who had rejected the women because of their horrible smell, a punishment from Aphrodite for neglecting her cult. Hypsipyle had to flee the island when it was discovered she had saved her father but she was captured by pirates who sold her as a slave to King Lycurgus of Nemea. His young son, at this time, was a child in arms, but an oracle had pronounced a dreadful fate for the boy if he was laid upon the ground before he could walk.

When the army of the Seven against Thebes reached Nemea, it was in need of water and seeing Hypsipyle, asked her where they might find some. Without thinking, she placed the child on the ground and showed the soldiers a spring. Immediately the young prince was killed by the dragon who guarded the spring. Lycurgus, on hearing what had happened, was about to have Hypsipyle put to death when her two sons, by Jason, arrived looking for their mother. Amphiaraüs, one of the Seven, recognized them by the gold vine branch worn by one of the sons, Thasus, which had been given to him by Dionysus.

The army gave the small prince a splendid funeral and instituted games to be played at Nemea every two years. The games resembled those played at Delphi in so much that there were gymnastic, equestrian and musical events, and the prize was a wreath of parsley. The games were confined to the soldiers, at first, then to their descendants and were finally open to anyone.

This account of the founding of the Nemean games is based on Euripides's play *Hypsipyle* as is also the part played by Amphiaraüs, who renamed the child Archemerus 'Beginner of Death', his death being the first of the many lives lost upon expedition. It has been suggested by Nilsson that the importance of the funeral games and the association of a dragon or serpent and the predominant part being played by a nurse rather than the mother, point to a legend of Cretan origin, where child deities are common, often abandoned and associated with serpents.

XXXII

The Revenge of Alcmaeon

When Amphiaraüs failed to return from Thebes, his son Alcmaeon took part in a second expedition against Thebes, accompanied by the sons of the other men who had been defeated in the first expedition. This was called the Campaign of the Epigoni, or Young Heroes. Like his father, Alcmaeon had not wished to take part but once again his mother was bribed into persuading her son to go - now with Harmonia's magic robe. This time, however, the campaign was successful and when Alcmaeon returned home, he went to Delphi to consult the oracle as to how he should treat his mother. His father, Amphiaraüs had previously made him promise to kill her if he did not return from the war, as it was her fault that he was forced to go. The oracle forewarned Alcmaeon that he must on no account fail to carry out his promise to do so and the sooner the deed was done the better. He therefore carried out his instructions and even though the deed was done with Apollo's approval, Alcmaeon was pursued by the Furies for his unnatural act.

The Furies function was to avenge crime, particularly offences against the family. They lived in Erebus, the darkest place in the Underworld and as protectresses of the social order, they punished all crimes likely to disturb that order. They also punished overweening pride or hubris; they forebade seers to foretell coming events too precisely, and punished murderers, since that endangered the stability of the social group or arranged to have them purified from blood guilt.

Distracted by the Furies, Alcmaeon went to his grandfather Oïcles and then to the court of Phegeus, King of Psophis in Arcadia. The King purified him and gave him his daughter, Arsinoë, in marriage. Alcmaeon gave Arsinoë the necklace and robe which Cadmus had originally given to Harmonia and they still proved to be very unlucky. As a result of helping Alcmaeon, the land of Psophis was made barren and the oracle decreed that Alcmaeon must again be purified of blood guilt, this time by the river god Acheloüs. There was difficulty in finding a suitable site on which to carry out the purification, as Alcmaeon had been told by the oracle to find land on which the sun had not shone, when he had killed his mother. Alcmaeon interpreted this to mean the mud which had been brought down by the river Acheloüs. This the river god purified and then gave him his daughter, Callirrhoë in marriage. But Callirrhoë demanded the necklace and robe of Harmonia as a condition of their living together. So Alcmaeon returned to King Phegeus and asked that Arsinoë should return the wedding presents he had given her, pretending that he wished to give them to Apollo in order to obtain a final pardon for his blood guilt. Phegeus permitted his daughter to return the gifts but one of Alcmaeon's servants revealed the real reason why his master wanted the gifts back. In anger, Phegeus ordered his two sons, Pronoüs and Agenor, to set a trap and kill Alcmaeon.

Callirrhoë had been having an affair with Zeus and when Alcmaeon was killed, she asked Zeus, as a favour, that her two boys, Acarnan and Amphoterus, who were still children, should grow immediately to manhood in order to avenge their father's death. Her request was granted by Zeus and the young men first killed Phegeus's sons and then Phegeus himself and his wife.

Callirrhoë took the robe and necklace, which had caused so much trouble, to Delphi and dedicated them to Apollo. Here they remained until the Phocian war, when they were stolen only to bring further misfortune to the thief.

XXXIII

The Trojan War

Troy was situated on a hill overlooking the plain of Ilium, the ancient name for Troy, where the Scamander river flowed into the sea. The city was founded circa 3200 B.C. and was well defended by thick walls. Indeed a series of forts had been built on the hill, each one stronger than the last. It guarded the trade routes to the Black Sea ports from whence came the grain that Greece needed for bread. As a result, it was in a strategic position and its ships could easily intercept passing traffic.

Troy would not have assumed such importance if the war against it by the Greek Achaeans had not been partly recorded in Homer's *Iliad*. Homer was Greece's first epic poet (that is if he existed as a distinct entity and was not an amalgam of writers). He did not record the whole of the Trojan War but only an episode in the tenth year culminating in the death and funeral of Hector, the most famous of the Trojan warriors. Homer is also the author of the *Odyssey*, the story of the arduous home-coming of Odysseus, one of the Greek Heroes. The rest of the tale of Troy is to be found in the classical authors, such as Euripides, Sophocles and Aeschylus. There is even an account in Herodotus, that Helen, for whose recapture the Trojan War was fought, never went to Troy with Paris but remained in Egypt where their ship had been driven by a storm after escaping from Sparta.

Classicists were uncertain whether Troy was a real city or one invented by Homer as a vehicle for his epic. However, in the 1870s the city was rediscovered and excavated by a German, Heinrich Schliemann, who found not one city but nine superimposed one upon another. It is thought that the one referred to by Homer, was number seven.

The story of how Paris became involved with Helen went thus: When Peleus, King of the Myrmidons at Phthia in Thessaly, got married to Thetis, a Nereid, on Mount Pelion, all the gods and goddesses were invited to their wedding because Thetis was an immortal. All, that is, except Eris (Strife). Enraged at being excluded from the wedding ceremony, Eris threw a golden apple among the guests which was inscribed "To the fairest". As a result, Hera, Athene and Aphrodite all claimed it for themselves. Zeus ordered Hermes to take the apple and the goddesses to Mount Ida and there let Paris judge which goddess should have the apple. Each one in turn tried to bribe Paris. Hera promised him dominion over mankind, particularly Asia; Athene promised him victory in war and Aphrodite promised him the most beautiful woman in the world as his wife; so Paris gave the golden apple to Aphrodite. Thus, it could be said that it was the fault of Zeus that the Trojan War took place.

The judgement of Paris.

Paris was the second son of King Priam of Troy and his wife Hecuba. Before his birth, Hecuba had a dream in which she brought forth a firebrand, the flames from which engulfed the city of Troy and consumed it. As a result of this prophesy, when the child was born, he was abandoned on Mount Ida. Here he was found by a shepherd, who brought him up and gave him the name of Paris. As he grew up, he became skilled at defending the shepherds and their flocks, so he was nicknamed 'Alexander', meaning champion. Somehow, Paris found out who his real parents were and so was recognized by Priam as his son. In due course, Paris married a nymph, Oenone, daughter of the river god, Cebren, but he soon deserted her for Helen.

Helen was the daughter of Zeus and Leda. Leda was the wife of Tyndareus, King of Sparta. Altogether she had four children, Pollux and Helen by Zeus and Castor and Clytemnestra by Tyndareus. In spite of their different parentage, both Castor and Pollux qualified as Dioscuri, which means sons of Zeus, even though one was mortal and the other immortal. The boys were twins and among primitive people, the birth of twins was frequently regarded as unlucky. The brothers were the best of friends and did everything together. They rescued their sister Helen from Theseus, who abducted her when she was a child; they went on the Argonauts' expedition together; they carried off the two daughters of Leucippus and married them. This led to a dispute with the Aphareids to whom the girls had been promised and as a result, there was a fight in which Idas and Aphareus killed Castor. Pollux did not want to be separated from his brother, so Zeus turned them into stars, the constellation Gemini, the twins.

As Helen grew up she was besieged by suitors as she was very beautiful and Tyndareus made each one promise to help the one who was successful in winning her hand. He chose Menelaus, King of Sparta, to be her husband and they lived quietly together for some years and had a daughter, Hermione. Then one day, Paris visited Sparta and recognized Helen as the most beautiful woman in the world and when Menelaus went away, he abducted Helen. She was not at first attracted to Paris until Aphrodite put a spell on her, which caused her to fall in love with him. It was only then that she was persuaded to run away with him to Troy.

When Menelaus returned and found Helen gone, he enlisted the help of his brother Agamemnon, King of Mycenae, who was overlord of the Achaean cities in the Peloponnese, so that he had a number of rulers on whom he could call upon for assistance. A great fleet was raised and an expedition mounted to rescue Helen from Troy. Messengers were sent to all the principal heroes and rulers of Greece. Among the heroes were Achilles, commander of the Myrmidons, who was undoubtedly the most notable of the Greek warriors, also Ajax, son of Telemon, who commanded the Salamis contingent, Diomedes, son of Tydeus, the leader of the Aetolians, who had been one of Helen's suitors and a companion of Odysseus of Ithaca. Patroclus, friend and companion of Achilles was enlisted and old Nestor, King of Pylus, one of the best known heroes of the war, noted for his wisdom and much respected by the Greeks, even though he was past the age of fighting.

The fleet assembled at Aulis but was prevented from sailing by contrary winds. According to the seer, Calchas, these were caused by Artemis, who had been offended by Menelaus claiming that he was a better hunter than she was. Calchas said she could only be appeased by the sacrifice of Agamemnon's daughter, Iphigeneia. Accordingly, the girl was brought from Mycenae, on the pretext that she was to be married to Achilles. Just as the sacrifice was about to take place, Artemis was merciful. Substituting a hind, she snatched Iphigeneia and took her to the land of Taurians, where she made her one of her priestesses.

While the Greeks were waiting at Aulis, they observed a further portent. A serpent climbed into a tree where there was a birds' nest containing eight young birds, which it thereupon ate. It then caught and ate the mother bird, which had been fluttering around the nest. The Greeks asked Calchas, the seer, for the meaning of this and he told them that the war against Troy would take nine years but would end in the tenth year.

There are various accounts of the voyage to Troy, mostly belonging to the post-Homeric tradition but eventually the fleet arrived and the ships were drawn up on the beach before the city. There the Greeks made camp, ready for a long war. The city of Troy was virtually impregnable, siege engines had not yet been invented and the only way of taking a well-walled city was to cut it off from supplies of food and water. Thus, for the first nine years of the war, the Greeks raided the towns and lands of the neighbouring allies of the Trojans.

Opinion in Troy was divided about the war. Paris led the party in favour of war but one of the principal elders of the city, Antenor, led the peace party, as he strongly disapproved of Paris's action in abducting Helen. Aeneas, the founder of Rome, was also for peace. The principal warrior on the Trojan side was Hector, son of King Priam and Queen Hecuba. He was married to Andromache, daughter of Eëtion, King of Thebes in the Troad, whose city had been destroyed by the Greeks under Achilles. None of the other sons of Priam seem to have been of any importance apart from Troilus, who was killed by Achilles early on in the war.

The first casualty of the war was Protesilaüs, leader of the Thessalians, who was killed as he leapt ashore. There followed a series of raids and skirmishes between the Greeks and the Trojans over many years with successes on both sides. On the Greek side, a quarrel broke out between Agamemnon and Achilles, caused by Agamemnon giving Chryseïs, the daughter of Chryses, a priest of Apollo, as spoil after one of the skirmishes. Agamemnon refused to allow Chryseïs's father to pay ransom for her, so she implored Apollo to send a plague upon the Achaeans. Calchas, the seer, told the Achaeans that the plague would only be lifted when Agamemnon returned the girl to her father. This he did but in compensation he claimed another one, Briseïs, who had already been awarded to Achilles. In fury, Achilles withdrew from the war and sulked in his tent, which enabled the Trojans to drive the Greeks back to the shore, where in order to save their fleet, they were forced to build a protective wall. Agamemnon tried to make peace with Achilles and offered to return Briseïs and pay compensation. He also offered him one of the princesses of the House of Agamemnon without the bride price, provided Achilles would continue fighting but despite these offers, Achilles refused. Things went from bad to worse and Hector succeeded in breaching the defensive wall of the Greeks and setting one of their ships on fire. Whereupon Patroclus, Achilles great friend, persuaded Achilles to let him borrow his

Achilles and Ajax playing a board game.

armour and lead the Myrmidons in place of him. However, Patroclus was killed by Apollo disguised as a Trojan. Achilles, angered by the death of his friend, went unarmed to the gate of the Trojan camp and at the sound of his war cry, the Trojans fell back and allowed the body of Patroclus to be recovered. Achilles was now keen to resume fighting but Odysseus said that, first, he was to be properly compensated.

Having lost his armour when Patroclus was killed, Achilles's mother, Thetis, asked Hephaestus to make him a new suit. Once he was rearmed, he went into battle and in single combat killed Hector. Thereafter, Achilles gave Patroclus a splendid funeral, sacrificing not only sheep, cattle and horses but also some captive Trojans on the pyre. He caused a barrow to be raised over the remains, then games were held, starting with chariot-racing, followed by boxing (they did not fight barefisted but with their hands protected by ox-hide thongs wound round and round), wrestling and other sports.

108

Funeral games in honour of Patroclus.

Meanwhile, Achilles refused to give up Hector's body and dragged it round the walls of Troy at the back of his chariot until Thetis implored Zeus to intervene. Zeus suggested that King Priam take gifts to Achilles as ransom for Hector's body. So, accompanied by the god Hermes for protection, Priam took garments, four talents of gold, two tripods and a cup. Achilles agreed to give up the body to him and to refrain from attacking Troy for ten days: nine days for mourning and the tenth day for the funeral pyre. The Trojans were given safe conduct so that they could collect wood from Mount Ida for the pyre. Hector was buried in a golden chest, set in a narrow grave under a layer of stones beneath a barrow. The rites ended with a funeral feast in Priam's palace. "So ended

109

the funeral rites of Hector, tamer of horses". The *Iliad* ends with Hector's funeral, which is not given in so much detail as that of Patroclus but then Homer was not a Trojan.

Shortly afterwards, Achilles was killed, shot in the foot by Apollo, or some say, by Paris guided by Apollo. This was his weak spot as after his birth, his mother, Thetis, wishing to make him invincible, had dipped the child in the river Styx, holding him by his ankle, which she neglected to wet, thus leaving a vulnerable spot. Hence the meaning of 'Achilles' heel'. Achilles, too, was given a splendid funeral and was mourned by Thetis and her fellow Nereids and by all the Achaeans. According to Homer, Achilles went to the Underworld like all the other Heroes, but other sources say he was made an immortal. It had been foretold that Troy would only fall through the bloodline of Achilles, so after his death, the Greeks sent for his son, Neoptolemus, to help them.

But still the city held out. Finally, the Greeks resorted to a stratagem. They asked Epeius, an excellent craftsman, to build a large wooden horse, which he did with the aid of the goddess Athene. Inside were placed a hand-picked group of warriors. Then the Greek fleet sailed away out of sight, leaving behind a warrior named Sinon, who pretended he had been left behind by accident. On being questioned, Sinon told the Trojans that the huge wooden horse was an offering to Athene and if they took it into the city it would make Troy invincible. The Greeks had purposely made the horse too large to go through the gates of Troy, so part of the walls had to be taken down to get it in.

Cassandra, daughter of King Priam, was a prophetess who no one listened to, and even though she warned that the horse was a trick, as usual, no one believed her. Laocoön, a priest of Apollo, also warned the Trojans against harbouring it and said the horse should be destroyed. However, he and his two sons were killed by a pair of giant serpents, who swam in from Tenedos - a scene frequently represented on Greek vase paintings. Despite the warnings, the Trojans pulled down part of their battlements and hauled the wooden horse inside the city. Lulled into a false sense of security, little watch was kept. The Greek fleet returned furtively and Sinon released the warriors from inside the wooden horse. Whereupon, the Greeks fell on the Trojans and destroyed them. Priam was cut

110

down in his palace, his children murdered and the city sacked. Hecuba and the other women were taken into captivity. Only Aeneas and a few others escaped. Troy had fallen.

XXXIV

Aeneas

After the fall of Troy, Aeneas escaped with the help of Aphrodite, who was said to have been his mother. He went first to Mount Ida, carrying his father, Anchises, on his shoulders and leading his small son, Askanius, by the hand. Then, together with some of the surviving Trojans, they set sail to look for a new land where they could find shelter.

First of all, Aeneas went to consult the oracle at Delos, who told him to go to the land of his forefathers. Remembering that Dardanus, who had been an ancestor of the Trojan royal house, was said to have come from Crete, they went there. When they arrived on the island, a plague broke out among them. The family gods appeared to Aeneas in a vision and told him that Dardanus had originally come from Italy and that was where he should go. So they left Crete and arrived in Epeirus, where Helenus, a son of Priam, was king. He had since married Andromache, the widow of Hector. Helenus gave Aeneas further instructions as to how to proceed on his journey and after various adventures, they reached Sicily, where Aeneas was hospitably received by his kinsman Acestes. Here Anchises died, worn out by his sufferings. After a year, Aeneas left Sicily and was driven by stormy winds to Carthage, on the coast of North Africa. Dido, the Queen of Carthage, fell in love with Aeneas and wanted him to stay and share her throne, but he was commanded by the gods to continue on to Italy. Aeneas returned to Sicily to celebrate the funeral games on the anniversary of his father's death.

The Trojan women, incited by Hera, set fire to some of his ships, in an attempt to stop Aeneas's wanderings, but leaving the weak and old under the protection of Acestes, Aeneas set sail for Italy with the best of his followers. They arrived at Laurentum, near the future site of Lavinium, where Aeneas made friends with Latinus, the king of that part of Italy. Latinus had been instructed by an oracle that he was to give his daughter, Lavinia, in marriage to a foreigner. But it was only after a battle in which he killed a rival suitor, Turnus, did Aeneas marry Lavinia and settle down to a long and happy life in the city named after her, Lavinium.

The story of Aeneas was related by the Roman poet, Virgil, in a poem called *The Aeneid* and the noblest Roman families would love to trace their descent from the Trojan settlers in Lavinium.

XXXV

Orestes

The story of Orestes is connected with the legend of the Trojan War.

Agamemnon, the commander of the Achaeans in the Trojan War, was married to Clytemnestra, having killed her first husband, Tantalus. They had three daughters, Iphigeneia, Electra and Chrysothemis, and a son Orestes. When Agamemnon finally returned to Mycenae after the war, he found that Clytemnestra had taken a lover, Aegisthus. Aegisthus, thereupon, killed Agamemnon and also Cassandra, who had been assigned to Agamemnon, as part of the spoils from Troy. Some writers implicate Clytemnestra in the murder of her husband, others say she was innocent. Electra saved Orestes from being killed by secretly taking him to Phocis, where their uncle Strophius lived, and Strophius brought him up with his own son Pylades.

When Orestes grew up he was ordered by Apollo to avenge the death of his father by killing both Aegisthus and Clytemnestra. First, Orestes went to the tomb of Agamemnon at Argos (why he was buried there and not at Mycenae, we do not know) and here he dedicated a lock of his hair. Then accompanied by Pylades, Orestes killed Aegisthus and Clytemnestra. After their murder, Orestes was haunted by the Fates and went mad. He fled to Delphi to seek absolution from Apollo and was ordered by the Pythian priestess to go to the land of the Tauroi by the Black Sea and bring back from there, an ancient wooden image of Artemis. Unknown to Orestes, this was the shrine of Artemis, situated above a cliff overlooking the sea, where his sister Iphigeneia had been taken by Artemis after she had been saved from being sacrificed by the Achaean army before their departure for Troy.

Accordingly, Orestes, with Pylades, set off to fetch the image

114

of Artemis. They went in a fifty-oared ship and when they arrived at the land of the Tauroi, they left the ship at anchor in a bay, while they went ashore. The Tauroi were of Scythian rather than Greek stock and had the unfortunate habit of executing strangers who arrived on their shores. Orestes and Pylades intended to hide until nightfall and only then to approach the temple, but whilst they were hiding in a cave, they were found by some herdsmen and taken prisoner and dragged to the temple of Artemis for sacrifice.

Fortunately, Iphigeneia recognized her brother Orestes from the ring he was wearing, which had belonged to Agamemnon. In order to save Orestes and Pylades, she explained to the king, Thoas, that as one of the prisoners was a matricide and the other had been his accomplice, they would have to undergo certain rites of purification, as in their present state they were quite unfit to be sacrificed to the goddess. Iphigeneia maintained she would have to take the two men, together with the wooden image of the goddess, which had been polluted by their presence, down to the sea to purify them. Meanwhile, Thoas was to see to the purification of the shrine itself. Instead of washing the image in the sea, Orestes, Iphigeneia and Pylades hastily embarked upon their ship and immediately put to sea. However, a sudden gale sprang up and the ship would have been forced back upon the rocky shore had not Poseidon, at the request of Athene, calmed the sea. However, the Fates still pursued Orestes, with a following wind.

The ship eventually arrived at the island of Sminthos, which belonged to Apollo. It was ruled by a man called Chryses, a priest of Apollo, and by his grandson, who had the same name. The grandson was said to be a son of Apollo but on further examination, he turned out to be a son of Agamemnon, therefore a half-brother of Orestes and Iphigeneia. Just at that moment, King Thoas arrived in pursuit of the fugitives but with the aid of Chryses, Thoas was killed. Orestes, Iphigeneia and Pylades sailed on to Attica where they erected a temple to Artemis and placed the wooden image inside.

Meanwhile, Aegisthus's son Aletes had usurped the throne of Mycenae believing that Orestes and Pylades had been sacrificed on the altar of Artemis, in the land of the Tauroi. Electra was not so certain her brother had perished and went to consult the Delphic Oracle. Here she saw Iphigeneia and was told it was she who had sacrificed Orestes. Electra was just about to blind Iphigeneia with a flaming brand from the altar fire, when Orestes entered and matters were explained. Then the children of Agamemnon returned to Mycenae, where Aletes was soon disposed of and Orestes took the crown.

With the help of the Phocians, Orestes added a large part of Arcadia to his Mycenaean dominions and after the death of Menelaus he succeeded to the throne of Sparta, and shortly after to the throne of Argos, whose king, Cylarabes, had died without issue. Orestes married first his cousin, Hermione, the daughter of Menelaus and Helen, by whom he had a son, Tisamenus. Then he married Erigone, the sister of Aletes by whom he had a son, Penthilus. In deference to instructions from the Delphic Oracle, Orestes finally left Mycenae for Arcadia, where he died at the age of seventy from a snake bite. He was buried at Tegea, but later, his bones were stolen and taken to Sparta because a prophesy predicted that without them, Sparta could never be victorious against the Tegeans. Tisamenus eventually succeeded his father but was soon driven out of Mycenae, Sparta and Argos by the sons of Heracles. What happened to Iphigeneia is uncertain; she either went to Megara or to Brauron, where Artemis was worshipped in the form of a bear.

XXXVI

The Odyssey

After the siege of Troy and its final capture, the Greeks set out to return home. They had various adventures on the way back, a storm having scattered the fleet wrecking many of the ships. Nestor arrived safely back at his palace outside Pylus, but not all were so lucky. Neoptolemus, son of Achilles, warned by Thetis went home overland. Menelaus escaped from the storm with part of his fleet and reached Egypt. Here, according to one source, he picked up Helen, who had remained in Egypt throughout the Trojan War and that it was her double who accompanied Paris to Troy. On leaving Egypt, Menelaus was becalmed and was only allowed to continue on his way after he had captured Proteus, the herdsman of the sea, who told him that he was delayed because he had not offered the requisite sacrifices to the gods before he left Egypt and the gods were angry. He, finally, arrived home, just in time to attend the funerals of Aegisthus and Clytemnestra.

The most famous story of the voyage home was that of Odysseus, related by Homer in the *Odyssey*. Odysseus was King of Ithaca and the son of Laertes. He was married to Penelope and had one son, Telemachus, who was only a child when Odysseus had left for the Trojan War. Odysseus was one of the foremost of the Achaean warriors and noted for his wisdom and cunning, but it is the story of his return voyage to Ithaca, accompanied by twelve ships, that made Odysseus famous.

His first adventure was with the Cicones. Here, Odysseus and his men sacked the city of Ismarus, seized much of the treasure, killed the inhabitants and their sheep and cattle and feasted on them, by the shore. Odysseus wanted his men to set sail at once but being drunk they refused and in the morning the Cicones, having got hold of reinforcements during the night, attacked Odysseus

117

and his men, killing six of them and driving the rest away. Zeus, in turn, was annoyed with Odysseus for sacking the city and summoned up a storm, which forced them to run for shelter in the nearest land. Here they waited two days and then set sail again. However, as they were rounding Malea, they were driven back by Boreas, the north wind, which drove them off course and past Cythera. For ten days, they were blown before the gale until they arrived at the land of the Lotus Eaters, an island that lay beyond the borders of the known world. Here the natives received the crews kindly and gave them some of the lotus flowers to eat. This resulted in them losing all memory of past events and their homes and making them wish to remain forever in Lotus Land. Odysseus had to bring them back forcibly to the ships and they sailed on, arriving next at the land of the Cyclops.

The Cyclops were giants who lived in caves. They did not cultivate the soil but kept extensive flocks and herds. They were immensely strong, with only one eye set in the middle of their foreheads. They were protected by Zeus, whom they had assisted at the beginning of the world in the war against the Titans. The island where they lived was pleasant and fertile with many wild goats and Odysseus's crew fell on these hungrily, killing seventy of them. After feasting on the goats, Odysseus and twelve of his ships' company went to one of the caves to see what manner of men lived on the island. He took with him a skin of wine and left the rest of his men to guard the ships. They had to wait in the cave for some time as the Cyclops was out pasturing his flock. In the cave, they found goats and sheep cheeses and ate some of these, and made a sacrifice. The men were anxious to return to their ships but Odysseus was determined to see what kind of man lived in the cave. Once evening came, the Cyclops returned, driving his animals and bringing a mass of firewood. He blocked the doorway of the cave with a huge stone that would have taken ten men to have moved and then killed two of Odysseus's men, ate them for supper and had two more for breakfast. He then drove out his flock and replaced the stone.

Odysseus had not been able to kill the Cyclops during the night as he realized that he and his men were not strong enough to move the stone and that with the Cyclops dead, they would be entombed in the cave and would eventually starve to death. The Cyclops had left a vast olive club in the cave. It was slowly drying out and Odysseus got his men to cut off about six feet of the wood and sharpen the end to a point and smooth it and harden it in the fire.

That evening, the Cyclops did exactly as he had done the night before, driving his animals into the cave and blocking the opening with the stone. After he had eaten another two of Odysseus's men for supper, Odysseus offered him some wine from his wine-skin and went on plying him with it until he was thoroughly drunk. At one point, the Cyclops asked Odysseus his name and Odysseus replied, "No Man". When the Cyclops had fallen into a drunken stupor, Odysseus and his remaining men took the sharpened stake and drove it into his single eye. Blinded, the Cyclops called out for help from his compatriots but when they asked him what the matter was, he replied that No Man had attacked him, so they went away, thinking he had had some kind of fit.

Odysseus gouging out the single eye of Polyphemus, the Cyclops.

The next morning, he rolled away the stone and let his animals out. Meanwhile, Odysseus had tied the sheep together in pairs and placed his men underneath while he himself grasped the undercoat of an old ram. In this way, Odysseus and his men were able to get out of the cave unnoticed because although the Cyclops passed his hands over the coats of his animals, he did not feel underneath. Once back on board his ship, Odysseus shouted his real name to the Cyclops and taunted him. The Cyclops flung huge rocks at the ship but fortunately failed to hit it and by rowing hard, they got away. The Cyclops, who was called Polyphemus, then prayed to his father, Poseidon, not to allow Odysseus to return home or if he was to, to return alone and in a disconsolate state.

Next, the travellers came to the island of Aeolus, the Wind God. He lived there with his six sons and six daughters, and they entertained Odysseus most hospitably. As a parting present, he gave Odysseus a bag containing all the winds, except the one that would blow him home. So on they sailed and came within sight of Ithaca. Odysseus, who had been at the helm ever since they had left the island of Aeolus, fell asleep from pure exhaustion. His crew, thinking the bag contained treasure, immediately tore it open, whereupon all the winds rushed out, blowing them back to the island of Aeolus, where the King of the Winds thinking they were too stupid to be helped, refused to aid them.

The next place at which they arrived was the country of the Laestrygonians. They were giant cannibals, who sank all of Odysseus's ships except his, and ate their crews. Fortunately, Odysseus and his crew managed to escape to the island of the enchantress Circe, sister of Medea. He sent half his crew to spy out the land, where they were caught by Circe who turned them into swine with a magical draught. On going to search for them, Odysseus met Hermes, who helped him with an antidote. Secure with this, Odysseus so frightened Circe that she turned the swine back into men. However, Circe forced Odysseus to live with her for a year, at the end of which time he demanded to be shown the way home. To his horror, he was informed that he would have to go to the Underworld and find out from the ghost of Teiresias, the Theban seer, the right route. This he did and met the ghost of his mother, Anticleia, who had died since his departure for Troy. He also discovered that his wife had been besieged by unwanted suitors, all of whom were after his kingdom. Returning to Circe's island, he set off for home.

Odysseus and his crew managed to pass the dwelling place of the Sirens. They sang so sweetly that the sailors could not resist wanting to join them, but Odysseus avoided this happening by filling his men's ears with wax and having himself tied to the mast, so that though he could hear their song, he could do nothing about it. They then had to sail between Scylla and Charybdis, off Sicily. Scylla was a beast who lurked behind a rock and devoured sailors and Charybdis, a monster who lived under water dragging ships into her whirlpool. Scylla succeeded in carrying off six of Odysseus's crew.

Odysseus and the Sirens.

The island of Thrinacia, which belonged to Helius, was the next place they came to. Here the crew killed some of the Sun God's sacred herd, in spite of being warned not to by Circe. As a result

121

of such sacrilege, Zeus destroyed their ship with a thunderbolt. Odysseus saved himself by clinging to a spar but his men were drowned and he ended up on the island of Calypso, an Atlantid, who detained him for seven years. But even though she offered to make him immortal like herself, Odysseus refused to desert his wife and finally, at the command of Zeus, she let him go.

Odysseus got as far as the island of Scherie, when he was perceived by Poseidon. Poseidon had been away at a banquet with the Ethiopians and had not noticed Odysseus making his way home. Poseidon did not waste time before causing havoc. He raised a storm and Odysseus was wrecked yet once again. After floating in the sea for two days, he reached land and was rescued by Nausicaä, daughter of the King of the Phaeacians, who had come down to the shore to do the family washing. Odysseus was well-received and sent back to Ithaca in a magic ship of the Phaeacians.

On his arrival at Ithaca, he met Athene, who turned him into the likeness of an old man and it was in this form that he entered his own palace. He was only recognized by his old dog, who then promptly died. However, he made himself known to his son, Telemachus, and a couple of old retainers. His wife Penelope was still having difficulty with her suitors, who were rulers of neighbouring islands wishing to annex Ithaca by marrying her. She had until then succeeded in warding them off by saying she would choose one of them, when she had finished weaving the web she was working on. However, every night she unpicked the work she had done during the day, and thus it was never finished.

Once Odysseus had revealed himself to Penelope, she sought his advice on how to deal with her suitors. Odysseus told her to say she would marry the one who could string her husband's bow. They all failed and then Odysseus, in his guise as an old man, asked if he could try. He succeeded at once and shot the chief suitor dead. After a fierce struggle, more of them were slain and Athene had to intervene to stop the ensuing blood feud.

Here the Odyssey ends. Over the years, various stories have been tacked on but we shall leave Odysseus, safely back in his island, reunited with his wife and son and his old father, Laertes. One cannot help feeling that most of his troubles were brought on by himself and the intransigence of his men.

XXXVII

The Story of Tereus, Procne and Philomela

This is a tale of Thrace, a state which lay on the border of the Greek world.

Pandion, King of Athens, had two daughters, Procne and Philomela. They were great friends and did everything together. When a war broke out between Thebes and Athens over a boundary dispute, Pandion asked Tereus, King of Thrace, for his assistance and owing to Thracian help, Athens won the war. In gratitude, Pandion gave Tereus his daughter Procne in marriage. It was a loveless union and the Goddess Hera did not bless either the marriage feast or the birth of their son, Itys, a year later. Instead, a bird of ill-omen, the screech-owl, settled on the roof and screeched.

Procne was very lonely in her Thracian home and missed her sister Philomela greatly, so she asked her husband if she could visit her. Tereus agreed and went to Athens to collect Philomela, travelling by boat, which was much easier in Greece than a journey overland.

King Pandion allowed Philomela to go, on the understanding that it should only be a short visit, as he was growing old and did not wish to be deprived of both his daughters. Unfortunately, Tereus fell violently in love with Philomela, as soon as he set eyes on her and when the ship reached Thrace he took her ashore and concealed her in an isolated hut in the woods. There he visited her and raped her and when she threatened to tell her sister, he bound her hand and foot and cut out her tongue, so that she would not be able to say what had happened. He then returned to the palace and told his wife that her sister had fallen ill and died on the voyage. Procne had no reason to disbelieve him, so she went into deep mourning and built a monument to her sister's memory, where she offered sacrifices to her sister's spirit.

A year passed by but Philomela was so closely guarded that she could not escape. However, there was a loom in the hut and her old nurse, who was with her, was able to go out and collect some wool. It was thus that on a white background, in purple wool, Philomela managed to weave an account of what had happened to her. When she had finished it, she sent her nurse to the palace with the picture and told her to show it to her sister. Procne received it and immediately understood the message. Enraged with her husband, she dressed her handmaidens as Bacchantes and with them, rushed through the woods as though possessed by Dionysus's frenzy. When they came to the hut where Procne was imprisoned, they swept aside the guards, trampling them underfoot, and set Philomela free. They then disguised her by covering her face, and brought her back to the palace.

While Procne was bewailing her sister's fate, her small son, Itys, came in and she realized that through him, she could be avenged on her husband. She killed the boy and with Philomela's help, prepared a meal for Tereus from the boy's body. After Tereus had eaten, he sent for his son and was horrified on being informed by his wife that he was already within him. When he fully understood what she meant, he was furious and drew his sword to slay them both, but the sisters escaped and as they ran, they grew wings and turned into birds, Philomela into a nightingale, as her name implies, and Procne into a swallow with traces of red on her breast signifying blood. Philomela spends her time in the woods forever singing of her sad fate. Tereus was also turned into a bird as he chased the sisters. He became a hoopoe wearing a crown of feathers in place of his real crown, with his sword changed into a sharp beak.

In the Roman version of the story, the sisters' birds are reversed. However, if this is done, the point of the Greek name for nightingale is lost.

124

XXXVIII

Phaethon

Phaethon was the son of the Sun God, Helius, and Clymene, the daughter of Oceanus and Tethys. Phaethon was brought up by his mother, who kept the identity of his father a secret from him until he reached adolescence. Once he knew, he became anxious for his father to recognize him and set off to look for him. Phaethon travelled a long way, through many distant lands, before he finally approached the home of his father, which he found to be a splendid palace with tall marble columns and a high roof gleaming with ivory. The palace had been decorated by Hephaestus, the metal-smith of the gods, who had used all his art to make it a splendid creation.

When Phaethon entered the palace, he could not get too close to the Sun God, as the light that he emitted was too strong for him to bear. His father was sitting on a golden throne, wearing a purple robe. On either side of him were the gods of the Days, the Months, the Years, the Hours and the Centuries. The seasons, too, were represented: Spring, crowned as usual with flowers; Summer, with gifts of the harvest and sheaves of corn; Autumn, garlanded with grapes and stained with wine juice, and Winter was represent-ed as an old man with white hair and a beard. Helius recognized his son immediately and greeted him warmly. He hastened to put aside his burning rays so that his son could approach him and then he offered him anything he would like. No sooner had the offer been made than Phaethon asked if he could drive the chariot of the sun for a single day, as this would demonstrate that he was really the son of Helius.

Immediately, Helius regretted his offer and tried to persuade Phaethon to give up the idea, but with no success. He pointed out that Phaethon was not strong enough and that he was asking for powers which belonged to the gods and not to mortals. He explained the dangers of the route. The first part consisted of a steep incline, which was difficult for the horses. Even though they started fresh, they could hardly pull the chariot up the ascent. The second part of the journey was through the upper part of the sky and from this height even the Sun God feared to look down for fear that if he did, he would become dizzy and fall. The third part was a steep descent and as a result it was difficult to keep the horses on course. The Sun God also warned Phaethon that the sky itself moved and it was hard to struggle against this and easy to be forced off the path. Then there was the danger of falling into the sea and various other hazards, like the dangerous constellations, the Bull, the Lion, the Crab and the Scorpion, all of whom would endeavour to attack the sun-chariot as it passed by and which must be carefully avoided. However, the horses were the main problem. Even the Sun himself had trouble in controlling them. Having pointed out all these dangers, Helius begged his son to ask some other favour, but Phaethon was adamant. So Helius took him to where the Hours were harnessing the horses, anointed him so that his face would not be scorched by the glare from the sun, begged him to keep a firm hand on the reins and told him not to drive too low or he would burn up the earth.

Phaethon leapt eagerly into the chariot and took the reins of the four winged horses, who were called Flame, Fire, Brilliant and Dawn. He was very much lighter than his father so that the horses immediately felt that there was no restraining weight in the chariot behind them. As a result they quickly got out of hand. The chariot began to sway madly from side to side as there was not enough to hold it down and keep it steady. The horses soon left the well-worn track and set off in a different direction. Phaethon was neither able to control them nor did he know the right road to take.

Out of control, the horses rushed into the upper heavens and then veered down towards the earth. Selene, the Moon Goddess, was amazed to see the chariot of the sun wheeling far below her, when it should have been far above. As a result of the sun being too close to the earth, many of the walled cities were destroyed by fire, the forests caught light and the tall mountains became blazing infernos. According to tradition, it was this scorching by the sun that gave the Ethiopians their black skins. Wherever Phaethon

126

looked, he saw only devastation. Smoke from the burning forests engulfed the chariot and impeded his view and the metal of the chariot got red hot. The Nile withdrew to the heart of Africa and no longer flowed on its customary course through Egypt. Its mouth dried up and crops were destroyed. The earth began to crack with the sun's heat. Then Gaea, the Earth Mother, came and spoke to Zeus, asking him to do something to prevent these terrible things happening. So Zeus took one of his thunderbolts and unleashed it on Phaethon, who fell in flames from the sun's chariot into the river Eridanus (now the river Po). Here, the nymphs of the river took pity on him and buried his body on the banks of the river.

His three sisters the Heliades, Merope, Helia and Phoebe came looking for him and on finding his grave by the Eridanus, sat down and wept. They remained weeping and lamenting until their feet took root in the ground and they became trees. Their tears which had been unceasing, solidified into amber. The trees were said to have been poplars.

Pliny when he wrote his Natural History, had some doubts about this story and no wonder, for amber is made from the resin of one variety of pine tree, *Pinus succinfera*. It grew in the Early Eocene period, in the northern part of Europe, in the area now covered by the Baltic Sea.

XXXIX

Midas, King of Phrygia

Midas was the son of Cybele and Gordius, the King of Phrygia, a state in Asia Minor. When Midas became king, he was noted in the Ancient World for his riches. Due to his kindness to Silenus, the Satyr and teacher of Dionysus, the god granted him one wish. Midas chose that everything he touched should turn to gold. His wish was granted but Midas soon found unexpected disadvantages. He was unable to eat anything, as even his food turned to gold as soon as he touched it. He, therefore, implored Dionysus to take back his gift. Dionysus took pity on him and agreed to help him. He instructed Midas to cleanse himself in the Pactolus river near Mount Tmolus. The waters saved Midas, though the river was to bear gold in its sand ever after.

Midas was not so lucky with Apollo, the God of Light and Music. Pan, the God of Woods and Animals, had made a flute of reeds and Midas thought he was the greatest musician in the world. As the nymphs also enjoyed his playing, Pan began to think that perhaps he was indeed the best and went so far as to challenge Apollo to a contest of skills. As the contest was to be held near Phrygia, the gods chose the ruler of Mount Tmolus to be the judge. He was an old man with a long white beard and white hair. Midas sat beside him on his right hand. Apollo arrived for the contest dressed in his best gold tunic, carrying his shining lyre, while Pan wore, as usual, his goatskin, sporting his pipes. Pan played first and his music resembled that of the rivers bounding down the moun-tains and the birds singing and the wind blowing through the trees but it was rather primitive and wild. When Pan had finished, Apollo stepped forward. Pan's music had been evocative, but Apollo's was far more appealing. He played so beautifully that his audience was moved to tears. All except Midas that is, who loudly proclaimed that he preferred the music of Pan. This was too much for Apollo, who punished him by giving him ass's ears, to show that he had not made correct use of the ears he had.

King Midas was terribly upset. He retired to his room in the palace and ordered the court barber to make him a wig that would hide his ass's ears. This the barber did and the king was able to disguise his ears. However, he threatened the barber that if he ever breathed a word to anyone of what he had seen, he would have him killed. However, the secret preyed on the barber's mind so much that he could not eat or sleep for thinking of the king's ears. At last he could not stand the strain any longer and one night, when everyone was in bed asleep, he got up and went out into the palace grounds. On reaching the lake, he knelt down and dug a hole by the edge, whispering into the hole, "King Midas has ass's ears". He then went back to bed and felt much better. However, over the place where the hole had been, grew up a cluster of hollow reeds and when the wind blew through them, the words were heard, "King Midas has ass's ears". Soon everyone knew the king's secret, but the barber could not be blamed because he had not told anyone of the secret with which he had been entrusted.

XL

The Foundation of Marseilles

Phocaea was a great maritime state, situated on the west coast of Asia Minor, the northernmost of the Ionian cities. The Phocaeans were Ionian Greeks and the founders of the Greek city of Massalia in 600 B.C., now known as Marseilles, in what was then Liguria. They did so, as they wished to found a trading port and staging post on the way to Spain, which was a long voyage for their un-decked ships. The Phocaean state did not have enough land for its expanding population, so they had to set up daughter colonies, like many other Greek states. The Etruscans had told them about Liguria where land was plentiful and the population sparse, so the Phocaeans had sent out an expedition to explore the area and dis-covered the mouth of the Rhone, a far greater river than anything they had ever seen in the Eastern Mediterranean.

The next year the Phocaeans returned, led by a merchant called Protis, and his friend Simos. Before they sailed, they consul-ted Artemis of the Ephesians, one of the leading deities and oracles of Ionia. Artemis appeared in a dream to a Phocaean woman called Aristarke and told her to follow the expedition as a priestess, taking with her a statue of the goddess.

The Ligurians were not so civilized as the Greeks. Their king was called Nannos and he lived in a rough, stone house surrounded by animals, rather like a poor farmstead. Nannos received the Greeks with great courtesy and told them he would consider their request for a grant of land on which to build a city, after his daughter's wedding feast, which was due to take place the following day. Nannos explained how his daughter would choose her pros-pective husband herself, at the feast, by walking round the table and offering wine to the man of her choice. All the leading Greeks attended the feast and to everybody's amazement, she put the cup of wine down in front of Protis. Nannos agreed to his daughter's choice and for her dowry he gave her a wide stretch of land by the sea with a deep, safe anchorage. Whilst Nannos continued to live, relations between the Greeks and the Ligurians were good.

Nannos was succeeded by his son Comanos. Now Comanos had been told a fable by a Ligurian which unfolded like this: A bitch asked a landowner to lend her a stable for a while as she was about to have a litter of puppies and unless she could get shelter for them, they would die of cold, as the winter was icy. The landowner told her to go into his barn and make herself at home. When he returned a few days later, he saw six tiny puppies asleep beside their mother. "Must I go away now," cried the bitch, "see how weak and small they are. Do let us stay here a little longer". Six months later, the landowner wanted his barn back but by then the bitch was surrounded by six young mastiffs, growling and snarling. She said to the landowner, "Try and drive us out of here if you dare". Comanos construed the fable as referring to the Greeks and thought things over.

The Phocaeans were due to hold one of their national festivals and the Ligurians asked to be invited, offering to cut wreaths, branches and flowers, which they loaded into carts and took to the town. Now Comanos had a niece, who was in love with one of the Greeks. Despite a strict watch being kept on her by her parents, the couple managed to meet regularly but on the morning of the feast, the girl went to her lover in an alarmed state and said, "You are all in great danger. My uncle Comanos intends to murder all of you. He is hiding nearby with his army; the carts are full of his soldiers hiding under the branches and each of your guests is armed beneath his festival garments. Tonight, when you are all drunk, the Ligurians will rise up and kill you all". The young man went straight to Protis and told him of the plot and all the conspirators were caught and killed. It is said that Comanos lost over seven thousand of his army and was killed himself. This is why a law was passed decreeing that in Massalia, at festival times, the gates should be kept closed and sentries stationed along the walls.

The area around Massalia was called Gallia Narbinensis and Massalia became one of the most important commercial cities in the ancient world. Its inhabitants set up schools of literature and philosophy. Later during the civil wars between Caesar and Pompey, Massalia followed Pompey and in 49 B.C. Caesar besieged the city and after losing their fleet, they were obliged to submit to Caesar.

XLI

Croesus, King of Lydia

Croesus, son of Alyttes, was the last king of Lydia. He reigned between 560 and 546 B.C. Lydia was a rich kingdom through which the river Pactolus flowed, and was noted for its gold-bearing sands. The capital was Sardis. Croesus conquered the surrounding countries as far as the Halys river in Central Anatolia, and on the coast he controlled the Ionian cities. His riches were proverbial and Sardis became the centre of civilization and learning in the region.

One day, Croesus was visited by Solon, the celebrated Athenian lawgiver and as Croesus sought to impress Solon, he showed him all his treasure. Then he asked Solon to tell him who was the happiest man he had seen, expecting Solon to say Croesus. Instead, Solon cited an obscure Athenian, who had died in battle and been buried by the state. He named also, two citizens of Argos, who had carried their sick mother to the Temple of Hera and died of their exertions. Croesus was stupefied and maintained that it was surely he who must be the happiest man, Solon had ever known. To which Solon replied that the gods were often jealous and capable of harming men who sought to outdo them, and although he conceded that Croesus was happy now, he could not confirm that he would always be so. "Call no man happy until he is dead".

Now Croesus had two sons; one was born deaf and dumb and the other, Attis, was a good athlete and hunter. An oracle had foretold that the former would only speak when beset by a great misfortune, and the other would be killed by an iron-tipped weapon. From then onwards, Croesus tried to prevent the boy hunting and forbade him to go to war. However, a large boar came down from the mountains of Mysia and wrought havoc in the farmers' fields. The Mysians sent to Croesus, their overlord, for his best hunters

133

and especially for Attis to lead the hunt as he was considered lucky. Croesus was unwilling to send him in case he was harmed but Attis pointed out that the boar's tusks were made of ivory and therefore could not be the cause of his death. He reluctantly allowed the boy to go, putting him under the guardianship of Adrastus, the young prince of Phrygia, who had sought refuge at the court of Lydia after killing his brother accidentally. After a long hunt, the boar turned at bay and in the confusion of the final attack, Adrastus's javelin pierced Attis and he died. The young prince's body was burnt on a splendid funeral pyre with many rich offerings and his ashes buried under a tumulus. All this was more than Adrastus could bear and he stabbed himself beside the grave in remorse.

After the death of Attis, Croesus lived in semi-retirement until forced into action by the Persians, whose kingdom bordered his on the Halys river. Their new king, Cyrus, had plans to extend his realm and Croesus wondered whether to attack them at once, or wait. Before making up his mind, he consulted several oracles, sending messengers to Apollo at Delphi, Amun at Siwa, to Dodona with its talking oaks, the oracle of Apollo at Didyma and to the oracle of the hero, Amphiaraüs, with a test. Only two augured well; those of Delphi and Amphiaraüs. Croesus then sent them suitable gifts and asked them whether his own empire would last long. The answer came, "When a mule shall become king of the Medes, you may without shame take flight along the banks of the river Hermus, O Lydian".

Croesus then prepared for war. In the battle that followed, the Lydians were defeated by the Persians, their cavalry put to flight by the Persian camel corps, the like of which the Lydian horses had never seen before. Croesus withdrew to Sardis, a heavily defended city on a steep hill. The Persians laid siege to Sardis, and after a couple of weeks, a Lydian soldier who was leaning over the parapet, on the side of the city protected by a precipice, dropped his helmet. He let himself down the wall to the bottom of the cliff, retrieved his helmet and climbed back. A Persian, called Hyriad, observed all this and when a reward was offered to the first soldier to climb the ramparts, he decided to volunteer. He found the ascent comparatively easy and called to his companions to follow.

Thus it was that the Persians scaled the ramparts and captured Sardis. Croesus fought hard, accompanied by his deaf and dumb son, who upon seeing a Persian coming up behind his father shouted, "Man don't kill Croesus". The prophecy thus came true; the boy had recovered his speech under duress.

Croesus was captured and led in chains before Cyrus and condemned to be burnt alive. On the pyre, the king remembered Solon, who had foretold his downfall and kept muttering, "Solon, Solon". Cyrus wanted to know why he called this, but Croesus refused to explain beyond saying that Solon was a man whose advice was more profitable to kings than great wealth. Cyrus was interested and ordered the fire to be put out, but the wood was well alight and it was only after Croesus had prayed to Apollo that a rain storm put out the flames. Thereupon, Croesus dedicated his chains to Apollo, where they hung outside the sanctuary at Delphi. It was the Delphic oracle that told Croesus's messengers about the mule, which referred to Cyrus, the son of a Median princess and an obscure Persian. Cyrus was to keep Croesus as his friend and advisor for the rest of his life.

XLII

Polycrates of Samos

In the early days of Greek history, before the country developed into democracies, the Greek states were governed by kings. Some of these, like Agesilaus of Sparta, were good, others oppressed their subjects and became known as tyrants. Among the most notorious of these were Pisistratus in Athens, Cypselus in Corinth, Phidon in Argos and Polycrates of Samos. This story is about the latter.

Samos is a small wooded island, famous for its wine. It lies close to the Turkish coast, and so as to be able to rule it, Polycrates killed his elder brother and drove out the younger. He then strengthened the island's navy, building a number of fifty-oared galleys. He also engaged an army of mercenaries, consisting of one thousand archers, to enable him to prey on the surrounding islands and the mainland. At that time, Pythagorus, one of the greatest of Greek philosophers, lived in Samos but unable to endure Polycrates's unscrupulous behaviour, he was forced to leave and set up his school of philosophy at Croton in Italy.

Polycrates then extended his influence to the neighbouring islands and became a strong maritime power. He was regarded as a useful ally by other kings and Amasis of Egypt (XXVIth Dynasty) asked for his alliance.

However, Amasis was a religious man and he felt that Polycrates was pushing his luck too far, so he wrote him a letter: "My dear Polycrates, I am sure that the gods are becoming jealous, for everyone on whom fortune has lavished gifts too generously, comes to a bad end. You should therefore take precautions. Choose the thing that you like best and destroy it. If, after this sacrifice, you still have the misfortune to be lucky, resign yourself to a new sacrifice and even to a third one, if things continue in this way".

Polycrates was grateful for this advice. He pondered for a long time on which was his most precious possession and finally decided it was a gold-seal ring, beautifully carved by a well-known artist. So he put to sea in one of his ships and when he was several miles out, he threw the ring overboard, convinced he had thus avoided his fate and done all he could. A few days later, a fisherman caught an exceptionally large fish in his nets. It was so splendid he decided to give it to the king in the hope of a reward. Polycrates was delighted and arranged to have the fish cooked for dinner. When it was carved at table, imagine his surprise on finding in its stomach his gold seal-ring. On hearing this, Amasis was most upset and wrote another letter to Polycrates abrogating his treaty with Samos, "I cannot bear to remain the ally of a man whose good fortune is bound to expose him to many catastrophes. If some disaster overcame you, I should be obliged to come to your help. So let us sever all connections, for in this way I shall be able to witness your troubles with a quiet mind".

Soon after there was a rebellion against Polycrates and he asked Cambyses, the King of Persia, for help, suggesting the Persians should ask Samos for the loan of some of its ships, so that he could send the rebels among the crews and let Cambyses deal with them. This the Persians failed to do and the rebels sought help from Sparta. However, their speeches were so long and convoluted that the Spartans could not grasp what they wanted. Finally, they did agree to help them and laid siege to Samos. However, after some small successes, they were driven back and after forty days, they withdrew. Some say Polycrates bribed them with a newly minted set of spurious coinage (lead rolled in gold dust), but who knows. On occasions, Polycrates was too clever for his own good.

Meanwhile, under Polycrates, Samos had become a cultural centre. He did many great works, such as building the temple of Hera, and the water channel of Eupalinos, where water from the mountain springs was brought down to the plain through a great tunnel, still visible today. He also built a mole and substantial city walls. However, he made an enemy of Oretes, the Persian satrap of Sardis, by refusing to see his envoy. As a result, Oretes decided to overthrow Polycrates, who had meanwhile decided that nothing could go wrong with his ideas and planned to build an even larger fleet. This was not what the Persians wanted and Oretes was determined to put a stop to it. He sent Polycrates a message saying that he had fallen out with Cambyses and would like to join forces with Polycrates and bring all his treasure with him. He then played a trick on Polycrates's envoy, showing him treasure chests full of stones, which had gold dust on the top layer. Polycrates was completely taken in by the envoy's description of the treasure and went off to meet Oretes. His daughter warned him not to go to Oretes, as she had had a dream in which her father was killed and hanged, bathed by the rain and scorched by the sun. However, Polycrates did not believe her and threatened to punish her on his return. As soon as he arrived in Asia, he was killed by Oretes and thus his fate was fulfilled and his daughter's dream brought true.

XLIII

The Wild Man and the Prince

There was once a king and queen who had an only son. As kings go, he was poor and did not have a large army to defend his kingdom. This worried him very much, as he always imagined that other more powerful kings would come one day and take his land away from him.

As a result he grew sad and gloomy. He took long walks in the countryside round his palace, trying to think of a solution.

One day when he was out walking, he met a monk who asked him why he was looking worried. The king replied it was because he did not have a large army and he worried about what would happen to his kingdom if he were attacked. The monk told him that nearby in the hills lived a wild man, who was so strong that no one could withstand him, and that if he could capture him, his kingdom would be quite safe, as no one would dare to attack. The king was delighted and promised the monk anything he desired, if he could catch the Wild Man. He returned home and consulted his Twelve Counsellors, who were of the opinion that it would be a good idea to capture the Wild Man, but that it should be done by the monk who had suggested it.

Accordingly, the following day the king again took a walk and found the monk, exactly where he had been the previous day. The monk enquired what he proposed to do and the king replied that he had consulted his Twelve Counsellors, and that they were of the opinion that the only person who could capture the Wild Man was the person who had suggested doing so in the first place. The monk replied that he could do so, but that he required the gypsies that lived nearby to make a great copper chain and a very strong cage with thick iron bars in which to confine the strong man, when he had been captured.

The king, at once, returned home and gave orders that all the copper in the town should be collected to make the chain, and all the iron, to make the cage. The gypsies, who were the only ones in those days who could work metal, took a week to fulfil the task. When all was ready, the king put the monk in charge of his soldiers and sent them forth. When they arrived at the place where the Wild Man lived, they encircled the area with the chain and tried to catch him. At first they had no success, but after about six months, the Wild Man became exhausted at being continually chased and allowed himself to be ensnared in the chain and placed in the cage.

They returned to the palace amid great rejoicings. The king offered the monk anything he wanted, but the monk replied he only desired the love of the king, nothing more. The king loaded him with gifts before he departed. The king's misery was now changed to joy, as he felt that he could now withstand any attack that might be made upon him. He placed the cage containing the Wild Man in the Palace courtyard near the Palace steps.

One day, about a fortnight after the Wild Man had been captured, the little prince was playing with a golden apple on the palace steps. As he played, the apple slipped from his hand and rolled into the cage of the Wild Man. The boy ran to the cage and asked the Wild Man for his apple. The Wild Man, who had remained silent since his capture, said to the boy, "If you will get the key and open the cage I will give you back your apple". The boy, who did not know why the Wild Man was shut up, went willingly to the guardroom, took down the key of the cage from its hook and released the Wild Man, who gave him back his apple, then made off in the twinkling of an eye.

The king, who had been out, returned and as was his wont, went to rejoice over the Wild Man. Imagine his horror when he saw the cage open and the Wild Man gone. The king fell into a rage and went, sword in hand, to kill the guard. The guard, to save his life, told him that without his knowledge, the prince had taken the key and let the Wild Man out. The king, still in a temper, rushed into the palace intent on killing his son. The boy was only saved by his mother, who took him in her arms and besought the king to come to his senses, as did all the officials in the palace. In the turmoil, the prince made his escape and was hidden by his nurse. The king, when he had regained his composure, made an oath that he would never see the boy again. He had strained the resources of his kingdom to the utmost to capture the Wild Man and he swore that if he saw the boy about the place he would surely kill him.

The poor queen kept him hidden while she ordered for him an especially strong pair of shoes, into the lining of which she placed fifty gold sequins. She gave him some warm clothes and everything he might need for a long journey, and advised the prince to go and live in a foreign land until things blew over.

The prince set off and journeyed for one week, then two weeks; after the third week he came upon a swineherd who was tending his pigs. "Good day," said the prince, "Good day," said the swineherd, "What are you looking for here?" "My fortune," replied the prince. Then the swineherd told him that his indentures would be over in fifteen days and as he was weary of herding pigs, he would like to give it up. The boy said he would be glad to take it on, so in the evening the swineherd took him to see his master, told him that he wished to leave when his time was up, and that the boy would take his place. The master agreed, provided that for the next fifteen days the swineherd taught the boy all he needed to know and showed him the safest pasture to herd the pigs. In fifteen days, the boy had become a better herdsman than his predecessor. He was never idle and helped the master with the orchard and the good wife with the cleaning. The pigs thrived under his regime and became fat, for he brought good luck.

The master was delighted and wished to marry the boy to his daughter, but the boy remembered that he was a prince and that his mother had enjoined him to continue with his studies. So one day he went to his master with a long face, saying that he had received a message that his mother was very ill and that he must return home at once. The master tried to detain him, but it was no good and off the prince went. Again he travelled for some days, till he came to a town where, as he walked along a street, he saw a shoemaker. Here he pursued the same policy as he had with the swineherd, saying he was a poor boy seeking his fortune and so became apprenticed to the shoemaker. As before, he was a great success, working hard and pleasing his master. When he had been there for several months and the shoemaker had become very fond of him, he asked his master if he could learn to read and write, as he had forgotten all he had been taught, and his mother was keen that he should have some learning.

Luckily, the shoemaker knew a clever schoolmaster who was one of his customers, and he asked him if he could give the lad lessons, two hours a day. Next day, the boy went at noon to the schoolmaster's house and asked him what he should pay him. The schoolmaster was unwilling to take anything from him, but said it would be about forty piastres. The boy took off his shoe and took out one of the sequins that his mother had given him. (At that time Greece was under Turkish control, so the currency was Turkish.) The prince then made the schoolmaster give of his best so that in a short time he learnt all he could teach him. Then he hired a more learned man with the sequins from the other shoe.

This master also wished the prince to marry his daughter and become a partner, but again he made an excuse and took off. This time he met a goatherd in the hills and became a goatherd. As with the pigs, the goats prospered until one evening as the prince was driving them home to the fold, one goat strayed away from the rest. The boy followed it but it kept ahead of him, luring him on, but it was always just out of reach. When it finally stopped, high up on the mountain, the Wild Man appeared. He embraced and kissed the prince and said to him, "My Prince, it is for me that you have suffered all these years, but I have always been near you so that no ill will befall you. I shall now make you into a great king. It was I who enticed away the goat so that you might follow it. Now sit down and rest from your exertions." The prince told him that first he must go back and restore the goat to his master. So he took it back and told his master that he had received news from home that his presence was needed immediately, and he then went back to the Wild Man.

The Wild Man showed the prince a cave full of sequins and said they were all for him. He then took him to a slab of stone in the ground and when the slab was lifted there were three hundred steps leading down. The Wild Man told the prince that he must descend and, at the bottom, he would see forty chambers, in each of which was a Nereid. When he entered the first, the Nereid would greet him and ask him to marry her. He was advised to reply that he would willingly do so "with all his heart". She would, thereupon, be pleased to offer him a gift. He must do the same to the other thirty-nine Nereids and they would all give him gifts. In other words, he was to deceive them all.

All came to pass as the Wild Man had said. The first Nereid said, "May you shine as the sun," the second, "May you become a philosopher," and the third, "May you always be successful," and so on. The boy then climbed back up the three hundred steps and rejoined the Wild Man, who told him that nothing remained except to find the right wife for the prince.

142

In the next town, there was a beautiful princess who lived in a tower. She set all her suitors the task of leaping up to take away a ring she had tied to the top of the tower. If the suitor failed, his head was cut off. So many suitors had died, the tower was heavily decorated with heads and there was only space for one more left. The Wild Man told the prince that if he agreed, they would go to the tower and engage in the contest. He warned the prince that when he leapt into the air, he would slip a ring into his hand. He advised him not to pay any attention to the people, who would try and put him off entering into this unfair competition. Then he dressed the prince in a suitable outfit, instead of his goatherd's clothes and presented him with a beautiful gold mare who was as swift as the wind. They, then, both mounted her back and in no time at all were at the gates of the city, whereupon the Wild Man disappeared and the prince was left alone.

The people admired both the prince and his horse but were most unwilling that he should enter the contest. Even the princess tried to persuade him not to enter. The crowd followed him to the tower, crying as they went, "Poor dear prince". When the prince saw how high the tower was, his courage nearly failed him, but he was ashamed to admit it. He called on his mother for help and remembered what the Wild Man had said. He took a great leap and found the ring in his hand and the lamentations of the crowd turned to joy. And the prince and princess were soon betrothed.

Then the Wild Man told the prince that his father, the king, had been dead for six months and that there was another claimant to the throne so that he had better return home as soon as possible. The prince told the princess's father that he had urgent business at home and after exchanging rings with the princess, keeping the one he had won and giving her his own, they parted and the prince returned to his country.

When he arrived at the capital, he went to the palace and asked to see the queen. He was told that since the death of her husband, she had covered herself in seven black veils and refused to see any man. However, the prince pleaded that he had a very important secret to tell the queen, and this finally got him an audience. But when he rushed in and said he was her son, she remonstrated she had heard it all before and that men, all the time, were claiming to be her son. The prince repeated what had happened when he was a boy, about the Wild Man and how the apple had rolled into his cage, how he had taken the key and let the Wild Man out, but she was unconvinced, saying that that was common knowledge. Finally he told her about the fifty sequins she had put into his shoes, so that he could complete his studies. At that, the queen sat up and took notice. She cast off her black veils and threw herself upon him, saying, "In truth you are my son, you are my consolation". When it was known that the prince was back, the people ran to the palace and there was great rejoicing.

After a few days, the queen consented to go with the young prince to collect his new bride. And not a moment too soon, for she was wasting away, like a candle, thinking that he did not love her. When he arrived at the court, he was warmly received and the wedding was celebrated with great rejoicings. Then they returned to the kingdom of the young prince.

As soon as they arrived, the Wild Man appeared again, this time asking for fifty camels to bring back the treasure from the cave. When this was done, the Wild Man remained in residence to help the new king. Soon the neighbouring kings heard of all his wealth and good fortune and began to arm against him. Seven kings and seven princes came to fight against him with numerous soldiers. What could the young king do against so many? His heart almost failed him. But he was reassured by the Wild Man who said, "Do not worry, you have me and as long as I live you will have no need to fear anything". So the young king took courage and when the armies had come near to the border of his kingdom, the Wild Man arose and fell upon them and did not cease until he had destroyed them all. He took and bound the seven kings and the seven princes and led them before the young king, saying, "Here are your enemies, do with them what you like". The young king took pity on them and after telling them to pay him tribute every year, he released them, sparing their lives.

Eventually the young king became a great king, thanks to the help of the Wild Man and he lived happily for the rest of his life. And we more happily still.

XLIV

The Nereid

There was once a king and queen who had an only son. As soon as he grew up, his father died and the twelve Counsellors were anxious that he should marry a suitable bride. Various girls were presented but he did not like any of them. Now there lived near the palace a widow who had three beautiful daughters. The Queen became convinced that the prince must have fallen in love with one of them and that was the reason why he was so difficult to please.

She, therefore, asked the widow to send her one of her daughters to keep her company. The widow dressed the eldest up in her best dress and took her to the palace. The Queen received her warmly and took her to the Prince's room, saying, "My son does not seem to wish to marry anyone of my choice. Perhaps he is in love with one of you. If he tells you that he loves you I will marry you to him".

The girl waited, doing her embroidery but when the Prince came in, he took not the slightest notice of her and went to his table to write. Then he went away and the girl lay down on the sofa and slept till morning. When the queen came in and asked her how she had got on, the girl had to admit that the Prince had neither looked at her nor spoken to her, so the Queen gave her a ring and sent her home, asking her to send the second sister. This one was no more successful and again she was sent home with a handsome ring.

It was now the turn of the youngest daughter, Ianthe, who was not only more beautiful than her sisters but more clever. She had seen the young Prince and had fallen in love with him, so she decided to do all in her power to make him speak to her. When she got to the Prince's room she looked around to see what she could use. Hanging outside the window, she saw a cage with a singing bird in it, so she brought it in and set it on a stool near the sofa, next to a splendid candelabra holding many wax candles.

Presently the Prince came in and began to write, taking no notice of Ianthe. So she spoke to the bird and said, "Good evening little bird, won't you talk to me? Or you, my golden candlestick, won't you have a conversation with me?" Without looking up, the Prince said, "My candlestick, my candlestick, at your orders my candlestick". The girl did not like to say anything else, so she kept quiet and when the Prince had finished writing, he went away. In the morning, the Queen went to see what had happened. After all he had spoken, even if not to her, so Ianthe said, "When he came in, he wished me good evening and afterwards he asked who had brought me here and I told him the Queen had bid me keep him company".

The Queen was delighted and asked her to stay another night. That evening she again talked to the candlestick and the Prince answered the candlestick and once again when he had finished writing, went away. Her sisters who had expected her back, were not very pleased when she stayed at the palace. They were even more angry when they heard that the Prince had spoken to her and did not believe it and thought she was telling lies. As a test, they found a pedlar who had a pearl necklace for sale and asked Ianthe if she could get the Prince to buy it for her. So when the Prince came in that evening she told the candlestick about the pearls and the Prince replied, to the candlestick, "My candlestick, my candlestick, the keys are in the cupboard, the sequins are in the drawer, open it and take what you want". Then he sat down to his writing and after a while he went away.

In the morning, Ianthe told the Queen that she had been given money by the Prince to buy a pearl necklace and the Queen was delighted. When her sisters came, she gave them money for the pearls and they were furious and thought that the Queen must be buying them for her. So they obtained a pair of bracelets and went through the whole performance again and Ianthe bought them as well. Then the sisters said to her "If you are really going to be the queen, you should invite us to dinner so that we may meet the bridegroom, who will be our brother-in-law". Ianthe was very distressed at this request, but replied, "I will speak to him this evening when he returns, and if he is willing, why not?"

When she was alone she wept bitterly. What had happened to her sisters with whom she had always got on so well. Now they had turned on her like Lamias, as if they would devour her. When the Prince came in that evening, she had still not recovered her composure and was weeping. Thereupon he said, "Come here my dear candlestick, what is the matter that you are grieving so?"

The girl replied, "My sisters wish you to invite them to table my Prince but I have no authority here and I am in despair, so that is why I weep". The Prince replied, "My candlestick, my candlestick, the cooks are below, geese and ducks are in the yard in plenty. Go and prepare the table". Then he went away.

In the morning she went to the Queen and said, "My Queen, the Prince has ordered me to spread the table and invite my sisters to dinner. He also says that the cooks and hunters are below and that there are geese and ducks in plenty, and I am to order what I please. Will you give the orders my Queen?" The Queen replied, "Since the Prince has permitted you to do so, call the people yourself and give them their orders".

So Ianthe ordered the hunters to go hunting and she told the cooks to kill the ducks, geese and fowls and to prepare them for the next day, as she was going to give a dinner for her sisters. She was so beautiful and she spoke so pleasantly that everyone was pleased to carry out her wishes, but she realized that she could not get the Prince to table and therefore decided to dupe her sisters. With the help of the palace groom, she arranged that about noon when they would be sitting down to table in expectation of the Prince's arrival, he was to bring out the Prince's horse and to make a great clatter with its hoofs on the stones of the courtyard, which would be heard in the dining-room. He was then to send a servant to say to her, "Run downstairs little Queen for the Prince wishes to speak to you".

And so it worked out and the Queen was delighted that her son was once again eating in the palace but Ianthe's sisters thought the whole thing was a sham. When the sound of the horse's hoofs rose to their ears, they were very upset and when the servant came in and called Ianthe they could hardly believe it. Ianthe ran down the stairs and into the courtyard but she could not think what to do next and burst into tears. She sped to the cloisters and whilst pacing about she trod on a paving stone that moved and raising it she saw a staircase. She went down and saw a shed heaped with thistles and on them was the Prince asleep, and by his side a Nereid and a small child.

Ianthe returned to the palace, called the Queen and told her that the Prince would not be eating with them that day, but that he wanted two gold embroidered veils, one rose-coloured and one white, a silver comb and a gold embroidered coverlet of silk for a child's cradle, as a friend's wife had given birth and she wished to offer them presents. When the Queen brought them, Ianthe begged her to go and begin the meal, assuring her that she would come when she had taken the things to the Prince, who insisted she go to him alone.

Ianthe returned to where she had left the sleeping Prince. Spreading the golden coverlet on the ground, she placed the child upon it, picked the thistles out of his hair, combed it and spread the rose-coloured veil over him. She then removed the thistles from the Nereid's hair and covered her and the Prince with the white veil. Then she returned to the palace and sat down at table with her sisters and the Queen.

A Nereid.

148

When the Nereid woke up and saw herself and the child thus cared for, she turned to the Prince and said, "Who is she who has come here and done this thing to us?" The Prince replied that he did not know, "You know well that I can see no other woman but yourself". He then related how every evening he heard a woman talking to the candlestick but that he could not see her. Then the Nereid slapped him and said, "I strike you so that your sight may come again but I charge you on oath, only to take this woman for your wife". The Nereid clapped her hands and instantly a great whirlwind arose, just like that which had arisen one day when the Prince was out hunting. It bore her, the child and the bed of thistles away and a voice from out of the storm was heard to say, "You will never see me again".

The Prince mourned her passing but in the evening he went to his room and saw a beautiful young girl weeping. He told her to dry her tears and not to mention what she had seen. The Prince, who was overjoyed to be free, announced, "You have delivered me from the spell of the Nereid. Now let us go and kiss my mother's hand and tomorrow we shall hold our wedding". He led her to his mother and the next day there was great rejoicing when it was heard that the Prince was to be married. Everyone was pleased, except of course, the bride's sisters.

XLV

The Queen of the Gorgons

The Gorgons in classical literature were three frightful sisters called Stheno, Euryale and Medusa. They were the daughters of Phorcys and Ceto. Later tradition placed them in Libya. Instead of hair, their heads were covered with writhing serpents and they had wings, claws and large teeth.

The only mortal one was Medusa and, according to legend, she had once been a beautiful maiden but her hair was changed into serpents by Athene as a consequence of her having an affair with Poseidon, in one of Athene's temples. Medusa became the mother of Chrysaor and Pegasus, the winged horse. After the snakes were added, her head became so forbidding that everyone who saw it was turned to stone. Hence the great difficulty that Perseus had in killing her, when he tried to do so by seeking out her reflection in his shield. In later Greek folklore, the role of the Gorgons seems to have entirely changed. They became more like the Nereids, although no exact description of them exists. They can appear as beautiful women but may have another side to them, and like the Nereids are connected with whirlwinds.

There was once a king and queen who had an only son. Whereas the king was good, the prince was bad and ugly. The king had a vizier and the vizier had a son, who was as good and handsome as the prince was bad. They were of the same age but the prince took every chance that he could of ill-treating the vizier's son.

One day the vizier's son was out hunting with his tutor, when he saw, lying on the ground, a splendid golden feather. He asked his tutor whether or not he should pick it up. The tutor said that whatever he did he would regret; so he picked it up, put it in his cap and rode on. As they returned to the palace, the prince who was looking through his spyglass, saw something glinting in the sun. It was the feather in the vizier's son's cap. As soon as the vizier's son got back to the palace, the prince sent for him and asked him what he was wearing in his cap. The vizier's son told him that it

The Gorgon.

was only a feather and went and got it and offered it to the prince. But the prince said he was not interested in the feather; he wanted the bird from which it came. The youth went down to his tutor and bemoaned his fate and told him what the prince wanted. The tutor advised him to go to his father and ask his advice.

Upon hearing what had taken place, the vizier advised them to take some wineskins full of wine and go to a cistern in the forest, where many wild birds congregated. They were to drain the cistern, cut off the supply of water and fill the cistern with wine. This they did, then retired behind some bushes and watched. A beautiful golden eagle alighted, bathed in the wine, drank it and flew away, only to return later to drink some more. This time, when it tried to fly away, it could not, and was speedily captured by the vizier's son, who took it to the palace. You would have thought that the prince should have been delighted to receive the bird, but he was not. He fiercely resented the fact that it was the vizier's son who had caught it.

The Queen of the Gorgons and the Birds was out walking when she heard the news. In her distress, she tore off her girdle and flung it away and then shut herself in her palace to mourn, for she was very fond of the eagle.

After some time, the vizier's son and his tutor went out hunting again and as they were returning, they saw something shining in the grass under a tree. It was a broad, golden girdle with Gorgons and fishes represented upon it. The boy did not know what to do. Should he take it, or should he leave it. He decided to take it and put it on. And again, the prince saw it gleaming, as they returned. The prince asked to see the girdle, admired it and said to the youth, "Go and fetch the woman to whom the girdle belongs".

The vizier's son was very upset. He did not know what to do and as usual asked the advice of his tutor, who told him it was no use weeping, they had better see if they could find her. So they went back to where they had found the girdle and cast around to see if they could find anyone. On a small side road, in a deep valley, they came across a splendid palace, half-hidden in the woods. In the garden, a beautiful woman was walking alone. The youth called to his tutor and they rushed in and seized her. The youth put her on his horse and galloped back to the palace with her. On the way back, she contrived to break the pearl necklace that she was wearing, scattering the beads everywhere.

When the prince saw her, he immediately fell in love with her, but she refused to return his suit until all the pearls which were scattered on the road, had been returned to her. The vizier's son was sent to collect them. When he and the tutor came to the place where the pearls had been scattered, they found it was near a large ant-hill and the ants had carefully arranged the pearls in rows around it, so that it was quite easy to pick them up. When the beautiful woman (who was really the Queen of the Gorgons) counted them, none of them were missing. She demanded that whoever had caused her all these difficulties and pain be punished. The prince was only too glad to agree. She said an oven should be heated for seven days and nights and on the eighth day, the vizier's son should be placed inside, to be burnt alive.

The prince gave orders for this to be done, but there was consternation in the palace, as the youth was very popular with everybody.

The next day, the Queen of the Gorgons went for a walk by the sea-shore. The prince went with her and he heard her repeat many strange, magical words while she was walking, which the prince could not understand. When he asked her what she was doing, she replied, she was saying her prayers, so he left her. Meanwhile, the oven had been heating up for seven days but on the Queen's orders, the Gorgons were pouring water in at the back just as the scullions were piling wood on the front. Then the vizier's son was seized and put in the middle oven and left there all night. When the oven door was opened at dawn, he came out alive and well, because the oven was quite cool.

The Queen of the Gorgons then said that she had a trial for the prince to undergo to test his love. He, too, should undergo the trial by fire but for him the oven should only be heated for two hours. She explained that her parents had insisted that whoever she married must undergo the trial by fire. Privately the prince told the scullions to put very little wood on, so that the fire should not be too hot. After two hours, the middle oven was opened and the prince got in. As soon as he was inside, the Queen clapped her hands and the Gorgons piled on more wood. Soon the prince was burnt to a cinder. Whereupon the Queen hastened to the garden to the vizier's son, who was seated under a tree. She took his hand, then clapped her hands together and a whirlwind immediately whisked them away to her palace.

There, the Queen said to him, "Although you are young, you are brave and fit to rule with me over the Gorgons and the Birds. For I am their Queen. Because I loved you, I arranged with the Gorgons to bring water to cool the oven when you entered it. I also arranged they should bring fire to destroy the prince, as he was not worthy to live and reign after his father. If you want me for your wife, then marry me. If not, you are free to return to your own place". The Vizier's son readily agreed to marry her. The tutor, the vizier and his wife were all invited to the wedding and, for all I know, they are still ruling over the Gorgons and the Birds.

XLVI

The Three Citrons

Once upon a time there was a king and queen who had no children. This was a great grief to them. They prayed to God to give them a son and promised if they had one, they would build a fountain which would flow for three days with oil, three days with honey and three days with butter, and everyone could help themselves to what they required.

Within a year a son was born to them, but in their joy, they forgot their vow. One night the queen had a dream in which a woman came to her and said, "Your vow has been forgotten. Do you not know that I can take the child that I once gave to you?" The queen woke up in a fright and said to her husband, "We forgot the vow we made about the boy, that a fountain should run with oil, honey and butter for three days each". And so the king straight away ordered that a fountain with three mouths be set up in the courtyard and ordered the people to fill it with the requisite materials. This was done and for three days the fountain ran with oil, honey and butter.

When the three days had passed and the fountain had almost ceased to flow, an old woman, who lived some distance from the palace, came early in the morning to see if there was anything left, as she had only just heard of the bounty. She had a very small pot and just managed to fill it with butter. The little prince was watching from a window of the palace, and he threw a stone at the pot and all the butter was spilt. The old woman looked up and saw the prince and said, "I would curse you were you not too young to know what you have done, so I will but say, "May you not escape out of the hands of the Thrice-Noble". The prince never forgot the words of the old woman and puzzled over who the Thrice-Noble could be. When he grew up, he said to his mother that he wished to go and search for the Thrice-Noble. His parents tried to dissuade him but without success. Finally they gave him some money and a sword and let him go.

The prince set out, asking for the Thrice-Noble, far and wide, but no one had heard the name. After he had travelled through the cultivated land he arrived in the wilderness where he finally came to a large gate by the side of the road. He entered and upon seeing a Lamia swinging on the branch of an almond tree, said to her, "Good day my Lady". She replied, "Welcome my lad. If you had not wished me good day I would have devoured you". "Indeed," said the prince, "and if you had not wished me good day, I would have run you through with my sword". The Lamia laughed and asked him what he was doing in this out of the way place and who he was. The prince replied that he was a prince and that many years ago an old woman laid on him a curse that he would not escape out of the hands of the Thrice-Noble. Since then he had always wanted to find out who he was, and he asked her if she knew. The Lamia said that she had never heard of the Thrice-Noble but advised him to take the right-hand road and when he got to a fork, he would come to another gateway, like hers, where her sister lived. Here she advised the prince to wish her good day, and ask her if she knew who Thrice-Noble was.

The Lamia then took a fine silver comb out of her hair and gave it to the prince, asking him to give it to the other Lamia with her greetings. So he said farewell and travelled for several hours on the road that she had indicated. Then he saw another large gateway, and on entering, found a Lamia in a walnut tree. "Good day," he said and she replied as before, that if he had not greeted her she would have devoured him, to which he replied, "If you had not said 'Welcome boy', I would have run you through with my sword". The Lamia then asked him who he was and where he had come from? The prince gave her the silver comb with her sister's greetings and asked if she knew where the Thrice-Noble lived? She did not know either, but directed him to her other sister who lived in the mountains. "Take the left-hand road till you come to an old tumbledown cottage, inside a gateway. Enter and you will find my sister wiping out the oven with her breasts. Do not say anything but cut a piece off your cloak, wipe out the oven and put in her batch of bread. When the loaves are baked, draw them out and ask her what you want to know".

The prince did as he was told and when he had taken the loaves out of the oven, the third Lamia was very pleased with him and asked, "Where do you come from and what do you need in return for the service that you have done for me?" The prince replied, "My Lady, your sisters have sent you this iron comb,* with their

* History does not relate why this sister had an iron comb!

155

greetings and I want you to tell me the way to the dwelling of the Thrice-Noble". The Lamia replied, "My poor boy, I pity your youth. The dwelling of the Thrice-Noble is a palace of the Nereids. In the middle of the palace courtyard, is a Citron tree carrying three Citrons. And in them are the queens of the Nereids, three sisters. The tree, however, is guarded by two very fierce lions. I can give you some magic water which, when sprinkled on the gate, will cause it to open on its own. Nevertheless, you must provide yourself with four carcasses to feed to the lions. Throw down two of them, a little distance away, and the lions will eat them and not disturb you. Then climb the tree and pluck the Citrons. Then throw down the other two carcasses for the lions so that they will not molest you while you get down. I will deal with all the Nereids so that they cannot interfere with you. When you have the Citrons, do not open them until you arrive at a place where there is plenty of water or the queens will die".

The prince did as the Lamia had instructed. He climbed the tree, cut off the Citrons and tied them securely in his robe. He flung the carcasses to the lions, descended the tree and went on his way. As he went along the road, it occurred to him that perhaps there was nothing in the Citrons after all, so he cut one in half with his sword. Inside there was a beautiful maiden who called out, "Water, water!" and then died. He was most upset, buried her and went on. When he reached a small stream he cut open the second Citron, and the maiden inside also called out, "Water, water!" and died because there was not enough water to cover her entirely. The prince went on until he reached a large cistern full of water, then he broke open the last Citron and a maiden, Thrice-Noble, even more beautiful than the other two appeared. She immediately asked where her sisters were. He was unwilling to tell her they were dead and said he had left them on the tree. He wrapped her in his cloak and walked towards the city. Outside the city was a well and above it was a great cypress tree with spreading branches. He climbed into it and said to her, "I am a prince and it is my fate to marry you. You will be my queen, but now I must go to the palace and get you some clothes". He went off to the palace, told the king and queen of all his adventures and arranged for a carriage to bring the princess back to the palace. All this took time.

Meanwhile, Thrice-Noble had been sitting in the cypress tree. One of the servants, who was very dark-skinned, came to the well to draw water. She saw the reflection of Thrice-Noble in the water and thought it was her own reflection (remember that in those days they did not have many mirrors). She was delighted with her appearance and danced about saying, "As I am so beautiful, I won't do any more work". Thrice-Noble, up in the cypress tree saw and heard all this, and burst out laughing. The servant looked up and saw her, and called on her to come down. She refused, and said that she was waiting for the prince to take her to the palace. The servant said, "I do not care who you are waiting for, whether you want to or not, down you will come". She then climbed up the tree and flung Thrice-Noble into the well. Then she undressed and wrapped herself in the prince's cloak and waited for him to return. In a short time the prince arrived with the king and the queen. The prince climbed up and found something very different from the beautiful girl he had left. "How did you get like this?" he asked. "From grief," replied the servant, "You were so long in coming that I thought you had abandoned me, but now you have returned I shall soon grow white again". The prince was ashamed to show her to his parents, so he covered her up and put her in the carriage and they drove back to the palace. There he carried her upstairs and ordered special food and paid her great attention in the hope of turning her colour whiter, but with no effect. Meanwhile, another maiden went to the well to draw water, and into her bucket leapt a golden eel. She covered it with her kerchief and took it to the palace in a bucket. The prince was delighted with the eel and, much to the fury of the servant, spent all day in his apartments talking to it. The servant said that it was obvious that he did not like her, but preferred the company of an eel. Finally she declared that her skin would not improve until she had cooked the eel and eaten it. In order to please her he agreed, but threw the bones into the garden whereupon a beautiful lemon tree appeared the next morning.

The prince went to see the tree and it immediately raised its branches and threw blossom all over him. The prince was delighted and called for a seat and sat down under the lemon tree where he remained all day. This also did not please the servant girl and she asked that the tree be cut down. At first the prince refused but she persisted and so to get some peace, the prince let her do what she wanted. She set the gardener to root up the lemon tree and cut it up and throw the branches into the road so that the passers-by would take them away for firewood. Only the stump remained and this the gardener put in front of the fountain. An old man came to draw water and seeing the stump asked if he might have it for his fire. He took up his axe to chop it up but he had hardly struck a blow, when he heard a voice from inside the wood:

"Strike above and strike below,
In the middle strike no blow,
It can feel, for 'tis a maid,
And your blows pain sore her head".

On hearing this, the old man was afraid and hurried back to his house. Later, his son came in and said 'good day' to him, but the old man was so upset that he could not at first reply. Then he told his son how he had fetched the stump home for firewood and how when he had struck it, it had spoken. The son thought the old man was going crazy, so he took out his axe and went to cut up the stump himself. He struck the stump gently and immediately the voice spoke as before. However, when he struck where he was told, out sprang a beautiful maiden. She asked for some clothes and a white kerchief and some golden thread to embroider it with. Then she sat down and embroidered everything on the kerchief that had happened to her, how she had first become an eel, then a lemon tree and how the youth had rescued her from the stump and how she was now waiting in the old man's cottage. The youth took the kerchief to the palace as she requested, where he delivered it to the prince. The prince could hardly believe his eyes when he saw what was written on the kerchief. He gave the youth a handful of sequins and returned with him to his father's house.

There was a wonderful reunion and Thrice-Noble was delighted to see him. The prince returned to the palace to deal with the servant. He marched to her apartment at once, and began striding to and fro. She asked him what the matter was and if he was angry with her. He replied he had come to consider how to deal justice to a criminal. She said that perhaps she could help him as her father was King of the Nereids and often had to settle difficult cases. The prince continued, "There were a couple of lovers and a man planned to separate them and kill the maiden. What punishment should I give the man?" The servant replied, "My father had a similar case. We had four wild mules, so we tied his hands to two of the mules and his feet to the other two, and whipped them so that each took their own road, taking a bit of the man with them". The prince looked at her accusingly, "Prepare to receive your punishment. I shall not tie you to mules, but have you strangled". He then strode out of the palace and went back to collect Thrice-Noble, leaving orders for the servant to be strangled and thrown into the river. After giving a present to the old man, he took a carriage and returned with Thrice-Noble to the palace.

Next day the prince ordered the celebrations to begin. They had music and drums and great rejoicings. The prince was married to Thrice-Noble and as far as we know, they lived happily ever after. And we more happily still.

XLVII

The Tower of the Forty Dhrakos

Once there was an old woman, who had a useless son. He did nothing and refused to learn a trade. His name was Phiaka.

One day when Phiaka was sitting eating his lunch of bread and carob honey, a cloud of flies gathered round him. He struck out at them and with his left hand killed fifty. Then with his right hand, he killed one hundred. He thought to himself, what a brave man I am. I had no idea I was so strong. I will ask my mother for a suit of soldier's clothes, a spear, a shield, a sword and a bow and arrows, and I will go off to find my fortune. The widow was only too glad to get rid of him, so she bought what he needed. In a few days, all was ready and he mounted his horse and rode away.

After he had journeyed for about three months, he came to a forest at the entrance of which was a tower and in the tower lived forty Dhrakos. Nearby was a stream which emptied into a cistern. The water was clear and fresh, so the youth tied his horse to a plane tree and dipped his bread in the water and ate it with the cheese he had with him, and then lay down to sleep.

The Dhrakos were out, but when they got back at noon, they saw him lying by his horse under the plane tree, so they sent the youngest Dhrakos to investigate. He came back and said that there was a youth sleeping like the dead under the tree. One of the Dhrakos said, "That's lucky! We shall have a good meal tonight". But another Dhrakos said that it would be unfair to kill him while he was asleep: it would be better to wake him up and fight him. The eldest brother thought that would be wrong, too, but suggested that they could eat him if they could beat him at various feats. This they all agreed to do.

The youth woke up and was about to go on his way, when he saw a large number of tall, strong men coming towards him, whom he recognized as Dhrakos. He showed no fear but immediately girded his sword, rolled up his mattress and went to take down his

160

tent. When the Dhrakos arrived, they saw written on a scroll running round the tent, "Fifty with the left hand and one hundred with the right hand". The Dhrakos were a bit nonplussed but nevertheless, the eldest addressed the youth, "Here! You have come here without our leave and settled in our territory. We have come to say that if you can throw a ball as far as we can, you may marry our sister". Then the youngest Dhrako threw the ball and it crossed the river. The others followed suit, and they all went long distances. Then Phiaka threw a ball and it went as far as the mountains. "Our word is our word," said the eldest Dhrako, "The wedding shall be held in three days; but we must first go hunting, to have some game for the wedding feast". "Just as you like," said the youth.

The next day, the Dhrakos invited him to go hunting with them. They went to a place where forty-one roads met. The Dhrakos had been on forty of them before, but the forty-first was a road of ill-omen and no one who had gone down it had ever returned. The eldest Dhrako said, "Let us all put our rings under this stone and as we return from the chase, let each of us go to the stone and take his own ring and return to the tower". This they did, and the Dhrakos took the habitual roads and let Phiaka take the evil one. He continued up this road until he came to a reed-swamp, where there was a loud hissing coming from the reeds, and an enormous three-headed serpent emerged and slid towards him. The youth fitted an arrow in his bow and shot and wounded the serpent in the stomach. The serpent began to writhe and hiss; whereupon Phiaka approached and cut off its three heads. He then set fire to the reed beds and burnt them and the serpent's body. (This follows very closely one of the labours of Heracles.) He then went back to the stone and sat down to wait for the Dhrakos, who had not returned. When they did, he showed them the serpent's three heads and told them the story of the fight. They then all took their rings from under the stone and returned to the tower.

The next morning, the eldest Dhrako told the youth that they must ask their king to the wedding. Phiaka agreed, so he set off to invite him. The king received him well and asked after the bridegroom. The Dhrako said he was a valiant man and recounted all he had done. The king immediately said, "As he is such a hero, he could undoubtedly kill the wild boar, Kalathas, who has been ravaging our country. All the bravest Dhrakos have been sent against him, but they could not kill him". The Dhrako replied, "I am sure that he could kill the boar but neither I nor any of my brothers are brave enough to accompany him". "Never mind," said the king.

"When the wedding is over, I will write to you, threatening to kill you all if you do not kill the boar and if he loves your sister, he will be obliged to help you". For the king had heard that the sister of the Dhrakos was very beautiful and he was jealous that she had not been offered to him first. So he gave the Dhrako some presents for the bride and bridegroom and sent him home.

When the forty days of the wedding were over, the king wrote to the Dhrakos commanding them to go and bring back the wild boar, Kalathas, alive or dead. When the Dhrakos heard this, they were very upset and told their sister to ask her husband to help them. When he came back from the chase, she did so and he agreed. Next day he asked his brothers-in-law to go boar hunting.

They each took a horse, their bows and arrows and their spears. At noon they arrived at a lake and dismounted, to rest for a little in the shade. Soon they heard a crashing in the undergrowth and the boar burst through the rushes. Phiaka shot an arrow at it and hit it in the eye. Kalathas, mad with pain, rushed at the hunters. As he came near, the youth hit him on the head with his spear with such force that the boar reeled and fell to the ground. The youth cut off its head and gave it to his brothers-in-law so that they might present it to their king.

When the king received the head of Kalathas, he seemed to be very pleased and gave the Dhrakos many presents. Secretly, he sent an old woman to the Dhrakos's tower, to enquire about Phiaka's strength. She went, pretending to be a nun and asked the young wife how strong her husband was. The wife replied that he had often said he was so strong that if the world had a ring fastened in it, and he had somewhere to stand, he could lift the whole earth. The old woman said he should not boast so much, as in her country there was a strong champion, called Yiaso, who was stronger than her husband.

That night, when her husband returned from the chase, the Dhrakos's sister repeated all that the old woman had said. Immediately, Phiaka thought he had better make the acquaintance of Yiaso. Therefore, the next day, instead of going out to hunt, he buckled on his weapons and, telling his wife he would not be back for some time, set off to look for Yiaso. He journeyed for a month, asking everywhere if anyone knew the whereabouts of Yiaso. Eventually, he came to a town, where he was glad to hear that Yiaso lived. He searched for him throughout the town and finally found him in a cookshop. Having established that it was Yiaso, he discov-

ered that Yiaso knew all about him and what he had done. Yiaso proposed a trial of strength: it was to see who could drive the other furthest into the ground with a blow on the shoulder, and also who could lift a weight higher than the other. Depending upon who won, that man should be master. The weight test was a barrel, filled with lead. Yiaso took him to his house, picked up the barrel and lifted it as high as his knees. He then gave Phiaka a blow on the shoulder which drove him into the ground up to his knees. When Phiaka came to lift the barrel, he raised it as high as his chest and when he hit Yiaso on the shoulder, Yiaso sank into the earth up to his armpits.

Yiaso allowed that Phiaka was his master and they both went off together to the tower of the Dhrakos. The Dhrakos were delighted to see Phiaka and they told him that the king had sent a message, five or six days previously, to say that he was to go and get for the king the Water of Life. When Phiaka heard this, he was alarmed. Next morning he repeated the news to Yiaso, who said that there was a man in his country called Ear of the Earth, who would be able to help him. So Yiaso asked for a horse and went off to look for the man, for as he said, Ear of the Earth was a friend of his and would probably do him a favour. Next day he was given a fast horse and he set off. He was away for forty days and finally returned with Ear of the Earth, who was a strange-looking man, with long ears, rather like a donkey's, which had the power of hearing what men were talking about, in all parts of the world.

Ear of the Earth told them that the Waters of Life were kept far away in the East, between two mountains that opened and shut. When the mountains were open they were guarded by a Dhrako, and whoever would want the water must take a skin of Commandaria wine from Cyprus and give it to the Dhrako, who would not only enable them to pass through, but would also hold the mountains apart so they could get back from the well. Phiaka asked if Ear of the Earth and Yiaso would come with him, and they agreed. He then asked the Dhrakos to look after their sister while he was away. After five days of preparation, the three set forth on swift horses.

They travelled for many days; the land they passed through being wild and uninhabited. One evening Ear of the Earth, who had been listening intently, said that he could hear the Dhrako guarding the Water of Life, complaining that he had not tasted wine since King Alexander had come seeking the Water of Life. Finally, they approached near enough for Ear of the Earth to hear the guardian Dhrako snoring. At last they arrived and saw the Dhrako sitting under a plane tree. The Dhrako greeted them and asked them what they wanted. When they said that they wanted the Water of Life, he replied, "O my pallikari (young man), this mountain where the well of the Water of Life is, opens and shuts. I do not believe that you will be able to fill your bottle in time, and then you will be shut in. Nor do I think that your two companions are strong enough to hold open the mountains while you are filling your bottle". The youth asked him if he would hold open the mountains and the Dhrako replied that he was strong only when he drank. Phiaka pointed out that there was plenty of water, but the Dhrako said that the only thing that strengthened him was wine. When they heard that, they offered him a wineskin. The Dhrako's eyes sparkled with pleasure. After he had drunk some of the wine, he said, "Wait a little," and when the mountains opened, the Dhrako held them apart, until Phiaka had filled his bottle. The youth then thanked the Dhrako, told him that the rest of the wine in the skin was for him and bade him farewell. Then they set off on the return journey. Before they left, the Dhrako, who was delighted with his gift, gave Phiaka three horse hairs, one black, one white and one red. He told the youth that if ever he was in danger, he and his brothers would come to his help. He told Phiaka that he was the brother who guarded the Water of Life, another brother guarded the Red Apple Tree with the Golden Apples, and the third brother kept the Souls of the Dead at the mouth of Hades. The youth thanked the Dhrako, took the horse hairs and hastened to the Dhrakos's tower.

As they rode on their way, the Ear of the Earth said to Phiaka that the tower was surrounded by three hundred Dhrakos. Your brothers-in-law are fighting them off, but ten have been killed and five are badly wounded. The three hurried on as quickly as they could, and soon they saw the tower in the distance. They could hear the shouts of the besiegers and the defiance of the besieged. When the besiegers saw them arriving they ran away, for they were afraid of Phiaka.

Phiaka bathed the dead and wounded with the Water of Life and they all recovered. However, they were not left long in peace. After a few days, Ear of the Earth came to Phiaka and said that he could hear the tramp of many soldiers coming towards the tower. It was the army of the King of the Dhrakos, who was coming with his followers to take away Phiaka's bride. Three days later the garden was full of soldiers. One group set up their tents in the garden, one near the forest and a third by the river in the cornfields. Phiaka struck the horse hairs he had received from the Dhrako and within twenty-four hours a white cloud appeared in the East and a warrior, mounted on a Triton (half man, half fish), descended on the tower, holding in his hand a bottle containing the Water of Life. Then appeared a red cloud from the West, and a warrior mounted on a red horse, alighted on the tower, bearing a box containing a Golden Apple. When he had dismounted, there appeared a black cloud from the South and a warrior dressed all in black, on a black horse and bearing in his hand a harpesh (a sickle-shaped sword). This was the Dhrako guardian of Hades. After they had rested, they prepared for battle. The Dhrako of the Water of Life diverted the river into the field where the troops were encamped, drowning many, and the rest fled. The Dhrako who was guardian of the Red Apple Tree, set the forest on fire, near the second body of the enemy and many were burned, the rest fleeing. And finally the Dhrako who was Guardian of Hades, fell on the troops in the garden, killing most of them in the night and the rest fled. At dawn, the defenders of the tower joined in the fight and killed the King of the Dhrakos and everyone else who was left.

Phiaka was made king over the country of the Dhrakos and the three Dhrakos gave him the Golden Apple. All the Dhrakos who had been their friends were revived with the Water of Life. Then for eight days afterwards, they rejoiced at their victory. I left them well and came here and found you better.

XLVIII

The Strangler Princess

Once upon a time there was a king and queen, who had three sons, as fine young men as you would wish to see. However, they were not satisfied and wished for a daughter as well. In due time a baby girl was born, but the youngest son, on coming home, was alarmed to notice that his sister had eyes like stars and gripped his neck savagely with her baby fingers. This made him uneasy.

During the night, there was a great uproar in the stables. In the morning, the finest horse was found strangled and the following night, another. So the eldest prince decided to spend the night in the stables to see what happened, but nothing took place. The following night when no one was present another horse was strangled. The same thing occurred when the second prince kept watch but as soon as he stopped, the killings began again. When the youngest prince decided to take his turn, he told no one, and at midnight he saw his sister fling herself on the neck of a horse to kill it. The prince intervened and cut off her little finger. In the morning he told his parents and brothers that his sister was the strangler, but despite the evidence of the missing finger, they would not believe him and he was thrown out of the palace and told to leave the country.

The prince left and after walking for several days he arrived, tired and hungry, at a tower whose door stood open. On entering, he found a beautiful princess. She told him it was the home of forty Dhrakos, who had stolen her because of her beauty. She had seen nobody for four years. As they were talking, there was a noise like rushing wind and the girl gave the prince a slap and turned him into a broom, which she propped up behind the door. In came a Dhrako and sniffed, saying, "I smell the smell of a man". The princess said one had passed by some time ago on the road and the smell must have come in. In turn, all the other Dhrakos came in and said the same thing, but the princess put them off and gave them a meal before they went to bed. She then hung a red handkerchief out of the window, whereupon a young horseman appeared and asked her to go away with him. She replied they must wait, as God had sent them a prince, who would kill the Dhrakos, and whom she would send away to get the Water of Life. The horseman went away and the princess restored the prince to his proper shape. He asked her to marry him and she agreed on condition that he kill the forty Dhrakos. This he did as they came in, one by one, the next evening. Then the princess asked the prince to go and get the Water of Life, as the blood of the dead Drakos would otherwise strangle her within a year. She told him the water was in a far-away land and there would be many difficulties. She gave him a jar for the water and sent him on his way.

On the way, the prince came to a beautiful palace which belonged to a Nereid, who had three great dogs. She told him the way to the Water of Life. First he would come to a black mountain behind which was an even higher green mountain covered in snakes, for which she gave him a potion to protect him. Then she informed him that he would see a lake which he must cross in a little boat. On the other side was a mountain which opened and closed and the Nereid gave him a basket of doves, which he could release to see if it was safe to pass through. When he had managed to get the water, he was to come back and tell her. The prince set off and found everything as she had described it. He passed the mountain unharmed and filled the jar with the Water of Life and returned to the Nereid, who was surprised to see him so soon.

Now, because she was a Nereid she knew all about the princess and her young horseman and did not see why the prince should be destroyed by her. So she gave him a meal and while he rested, she changed the Water of Life in the jar for ordinary water. When he woke, the prince set out for the Dhrakos tower. After he had gone, the Nereid called her biggest dog, Arslán (Lion), and told him to follow the prince and watch over all that happened. The prince, meantime, had arrived at the tower where the princess was living happily with her young horseman. She saw him coming and gave him a glass of wine which contained a drug, which sent him to sleep. She then cut him in pieces, tied the bits in a sheet and flung them out of the window. The dog, Arslán, was waiting and taking the sheet in his mouth, ran back to his mistress. The Nereid carefully laid out every bit, carefully putting each piece in its proper place. Then she got a watermelon from the garden, cut it into thin slices, mixed it with the Water of Life and put it on the prince's wounds and poured the rest all over him. Soon he began to move

167

and to ask where he was. He rested for some days and it was not long before he was quite recovered. He returned to the tower and killed the wicked couple and agreed to marry the Nereid. Before doing so, however, he wanted to go home and see how his family had got on.

The Nereid gave him three dates and told him to eat them on the way and then plant the stones by the side of the road, whereupon they would grow into tall trees. She also announced that if he needed help he had to climb up the date trees and call her dogs, "Come my Arslán, Come my Kurd (Wolf), Come my Pars (Leopard)," and the dogs would be with him in the twinkling of an eye. All this the prince agreed to do. When he arrived at his native city, he found it like a ghost town, with no one about and all the houses shut up. He went to the palace and found Djinns playing ball in the courtyard. His father, now a poor legless old man, was lying in a corner and immediately called the Strangler Princess. She ran up and seized the prince, making him beat a drum while she sharpened her teeth so as to kill him quickly. Fortunately, a mouse saw the prince beating the drum and took over while the prince ran off. His sister ran after him and as she could run faster than he could, she had nearly caught up with him, when the first date tree came in sight. He climbed up, but in no time she had sawn through the trunk and he had to jump onto the next tree. When on the last tree, he called the dogs, "Come my Arslán, Come my Kurd, Come my Pars" and the dogs rushed up and tore the princess to pieces.

The prince returned, sorrowfully, to the Nereid and related everything that had happened. She accompanied him back to the palace, taking her servants. The prince issued a proclamation that the Strangler Princess had been destroyed and that the youngest prince had returned and would welcome back any of his subjects that had fled. Many returned home and the kingdom was enlarged by the territory that had originally belonged to the Dhrakos, and the prince and the Nereid lived happily for many years.

XLIX

The Chapel of Ayios Hilarios

An old peasant woman, all in black, was sitting in the curator's office, telling the curator that she had dreamt the same dream three nights running. "A chapel stood on the sea side of the present church and in my dream, it was all lit up and Ayios Hilarios was in the doorway beckoning to me". "Well," said the curator, "we will do something about it as soon as we can".

And so it was that, about a fortnight later, I found myself, with Lazarus the deputy foreman of the guards in the Cyprus Museum, going down a dusty track, leading off the main road to the village of Ayios Hilarios, on the east coast of the island. Maria, the old peasant woman, was waiting for us. "It is right here," she said, pointing to a dusty area between the present church and a bluff overlooking the small bay. Below the bluff was a cave and in the cave was a spring that never ran dry, however hot the summer. This was reputedly the work of Ayios Hilarios who, having found no water in the area, had struck the rock and water had gushed forth from a spring.

We laid out a grid and began work with the help of several villagers, anxious to see if there had really been an earlier chapel on the site. The trench nearest the bluff yielded, to our surprise, a vast quantity of bones. The villagers crossed themselves. "These are the bones of the ten thousand virgins," they said, "massacred by the Turks when they occupied the island after taking it from the Venetians in A.D. 1570". However, Lazarus was sceptical, "I do not think these are human bones," he said. So we took a sample back to Nicosia and showed them to an American anthropologist, who was working at the site of Curium.

After he had examined them, he said, "These are the bones of pigmy elephants. These vertebrates found their way to Cyprus in the Pleistocene, when there was a land bridge between Asia Minor and Cyprus. When the land bridge was cut, the elephants diminished in size, until they became pigmies and later extinct".

Meanwhile, work continued with our excavations. It was not long before we came upon some foundations at the side of which were a pile of stones, indicating that a little basilica had been destroyed by an earthquake.

So Maria's dream had been justified and in finding the bones of the pigmy elephants, we had added a little more knowledge to the island's history.

Glossary

Acropolis	Citadel or elevated part of a Greek city.
Agora	Greek market.
Aegis	Breastplate worn by Athene.
Ambrosia	The fabled food of the gods.
Dhrakos	In Greek stories, the Dhrakos seem to be the later equivalent of the Cyclops. They are usually shown to be very strong, rather stupid and with a weakness for eating human flesh. They possessed magical powers and often guarded springs and the Well of Life. In stories, they were usually overcome by the young prince or the widow's son.
Furies	Born from the blood of Cronus, they guarded the greatest sinners in the Afterworld. Snakes writhed in their hair and round their waists and they had the power of sending humans mad.
Gem-stone	Semi-precious stones, cut and engraved with religious or secular scenes.
Gorgon	One of three snake-haired sisters, so frightening in appearance that they could turn their beholders to stone.
Minotaur	A monster, half man, half bull, who lived in Crete.
Minyans	Greeks who settled in Orchomenus.
Nectar	The drink of the gods.
Nereids	The children of Nerus. Nereids occupy, in popular imagination, a similar position to fairies in Western countries save that they are fully grown. It was considered unlucky to speak of them by name and they were always referred to as 'the Outsiders' or 'the Beautiful ones'. They usually intermarried among themselves but occasionally took a mortal for a husband. They could cause storms and whirlwinds and had to be propitiated; offerings were made to them of honey cakes, milk and cheese to avoid the evil eye. Shepherds will bow in a gale, as otherwise they could be punished by the Nereids for lack of respect.

Oceanids	The descendants of Oceanus.
Oracle	The answer of a god or priest to a request for advice, also a prophecy.
Satyrs	Elemental spirits, with horns, pointed ears, a hairy body and cloven hooves. They delighted in chasing Nymphs.
Scylla and Charybdis	Scylla was a rock on the shore of the Straits of Messina in Italy (Homer described it as a monster who devoured sailors) and Charybdis was a whirlpool opposite Scylla. Hence a passage between the two was fraught with danger.
Sirens	Sea Nymphs, half woman, half bird, who lured sailors to their death.
Strangler or Stringler	Witches who made their presence felt in certain areas by strangling mortals and animals. They could be good but were usually bad and did a great deal of damage.

Bibliography

Garnett, L.M.J., *Greek Folk Tales*, Eliot Stock, London, 1885.

Garnett, L.M.J., *Greek Wonder Tales*, A. & C. Black, 1913.

Graves, R., *Greek Myths*, Cassel & Co., 1958.

Grimal, Pierre, *A Concise Dictionary of Classical Mythology*, Blackwell, 1990.

Harrison, J.E., *Progomena to the Study of Greek Religions*, C.U.P., 1922.

Hesiod, *The Homeric Hymns*, Loeb Edition, 1914.

Homer, *The Iliad*, Loeb Edition, 1928.

Homer, *The Odyssey*, Loeb Edition, 1928.

Kupper, G.H., *The Legends of Greece and Rome*, O.C. Heath & Co., London, 1910.

Lang, A., *Homeric Hymns*, George Allen, 1899.

Larousse, *Encyclopedia of Mythology*, Batchworth Press Ltd., 1959.

Nilssen, M.P., *A History of Greek Religion*, Clarendon Press, Oxford, 1925.

Otto, Walter, *The Homeric Gods*, Thames & Hudson, 1929.

Petiseus, A.H., *The Gods of Olympos*, Fischer Unwin, 1892.

Rose, H.J., *Handbook of Greek Mythology*, 3rd ed., Methuen, 1945.

Stampford, W.B., *Greek Tragedy and the Emotions*, Routledge and Kegan Paul, 1983.

Stassinopoulos, A. & Roloff, B., *The Gods of Greece*, Weidenfeld and Nicholson, 1983.

Warner, R., *Men and Gods*, Penguin Books, 1952.

Index

Achaean, 1, 4, 103, 106-107, 110, 114, 117
Achilles, 4, 7, 12, 43, 47, 57, 106-110, 117
Acropolis, 1-3, 26, 50, 62
Actaeon, 93
Adrastus, 97-99, 134
Aegean, 4, 52, 75
Aegeus, 52, 54
Aeneas, 107, 111-113
Aeolus, 120
Aeschylus, 96, 98, 103
Aether, 6
Africa, 39, 112, 127
Afterworld, 5, 68-69
Agamemnon, 106-107, 114-116
Agave, 86, 92
Ajax, 106
Alcmaeon, 98, 101-102
Alcmene, 33
Aleian Plain, 72
Aletes, 115-116
Althea, 56-58
Amasis, 136-137
Amazon, 38, 54, 71
American School, 3
Amphiaraüs, 97-98, 100-101, 134
Amykli, 3
Andromache, 107, 112
Andromeda, 64-65
Antigone, 96, 98-99
Aphrodite, 4-5, 9, 12, 59, 61, 66-70, 81-82, 99, 104-105, 112
Apollo, 2, 5, 9, 11-12, 17, 19, 23-26, 28, 37, 41, 47, 59, 73, 85, 94, 101-102, 107-108, 110, 114-115, 128, 134-135
Apollodorus, 38
Arachne, 62-63
Arcadia, 17, 27, 37, 101, 116
Ares, 5, 9, 11-12, 19, 38, 42, 85-86, 92
Argo, 3, 42-47, 56-57
Argolis, 5
Argonauts, 5, 37, 42-45, 47, 54, 98-99, 105
Argos, 1-2, 38, 50, 64-65, 71, 97-98, 114, 116, 133, 136
Argus, 19, 30-31, 42
Ariadne, 54-55, 78, 90

Artemis, 2, 4, 9, 11, 23, 27-28, 36-37, 56-57, 71, 93, 106, 114-116, 130
Asclepius, 47
Asia Minor, 4-5, 38, 61, 128, 130, 169
Asine, 1-2
Athamas, 87-88
Athene, 2, 5, 9, 11, 14, 33, 40, 50-51, 56, 62-64, 71, 77, 98, 104, 110, 115, 122, 150
Athens, 1-2, 5, 26, 45, 50, 52, 54, 57, 62, 77, 123, 136
Atlanta, 43, 57, 59, 61
Atlas, 14, 17, 39-40, 75
Attica, 5, 38, 50, 52, 54, 71, 89, 92, 96, 115
Aulis, 3, 106
Ayios Hilarios, 169

Bacchantes, 90, 92, 124
Baucis, 83-84
Bellerophon, 63, 71-72
Blegen, Carl, 3
Boar's Tusk Helmet, 1
Boeotia, 5, 26-27, 85, 87, 89, 92, 94, 96
Boeotian, 3
Boreas, 26, 118
British School, 3
Bronze Age, 13

Caesar, 132
Calchas, 106-107
Cadmus, 42, 44, 85-87, 89, 92-94, 101
Calliope, 27, 47
Callisto, 27
Calydon, 4, 34, 56, 58, 97
Calypso, 122
Cambyses, 137
Carthage, 112
Cassandra, 25, 110, 114
Cerberus, 11, 40-41, 68-69
Charon, 5, 48, 68-69
Cheiron, 36, 42, 47-48
Chimaera, 71
Chios, 44, 92
Circe, 120-121
Classical Period, 2, 5
Clio, 26

Colchis, 42, 44-46, 87
Comanos, 131
Corinth, 2, 45, 71, 87, 94, 96, 136
Corn Goddess, 2
Creon, 33, 45, 86, 95-96, 98-99
Croesus, 133-135
Cronus, 6-7, 13, 20, 36
Cybele, 61, 90, 128
Cyclades, 4, 64
Cyclops, 2, 6-7, 12, 118-120
Cyprus, 4, 59, 67, 81, 163, 169
Cythera, 118

Daedalus, 77-78
Danae, 64
Delos, 23-24, 112
Delphi, 25-26, 41, 66, 94, 101-102, 114, 134-135
Delphic Oracle, 26, 34, 66, 85, 94, 96, 116, 135
Demeter, 2, 9, 20-22, 56
Dhrako, 160-168
Dido, 112
Dionysus, 9, 12, 54, 56, 87, 89-90, 92, 100, 124, 128
Dorians, 4
Ducalion, 15

Echo, 79-80
Egypt, 32, 40, 90, 103, 117, 136
Eileithyia, 11
Electra, 114-116
Eleusis, 2, 22
Erebus, 6, 13, 101
Erechtion, 50, 62
Erigone, 89, 116
Eris, 104
Eros, 6, 66-70
Eteocles, 96-98
Etna, Mount, 8, 12, 21
Euboea, 3
Euripides, 5, 98, 100, 103
Europa, 16, 85
Eurydice, 47-48, 99
Eurystheus, King, 34-35, 37-41

Furies, 87, 101

Gaea, 6-8, 11-12, 25, 39-40, 87, 127
Galatea, 81-82
Ganymede, 9
Gla, 3
Golden Fleece, 3, 42, 44-47
Graces, 9
Greece, 1, 4-6, 9, 15, 17, 19-20, 26, 30, 39, 42, 45, 47, 50, 56, 62, 66-67, 71, 74-75, 83, 86, 90, 92, 103, 106, 123

Greek, 1-2, 4-5, 25, 32, 36, 43, 47, 62, 66, 68, 70, 75, 77, 86, 89, 92-93, 98, 103, 106, 110, 115, 124, 130, 136, 150
Greeks, 2, 5-6, 19-20, 73, 96, 106-107, 110, 117, 130-131
Gorgons, 63-65, 150, 152-153

Hades, 5, 9, 11, 19-22, 40, 48, 87, 92, 96, 98, 164-165
Hadrian, Emperor, 50
Halys, 133-134
Harmonia, 85-86, 101-102
Hathor, 32
Hebe, 9, 11, 41
Hecataetus, 5
Hector, 103, 107-110, 112
Hecuba, 105, 107, 111
Helen, 13, 103-107, 116-117
Helius, 9, 21, 39, 121, 125-126
Hephaestus, 9, 11-12, 14-15, 24, 37, 39, 44, 86, 97, 108, 125
Hera, 2, 5, 9, 11-12, 23-24, 30, 33, 38-42, 51, 75-76, 79, 87, 89, 104, 112, 123, 133, 137
Heracles, 1, 5, 8, 17, 19, 33-41, 43-44, 47, 54, 63, 73-74, 116, 161
Heraion, 2
Hermes, 2, 9, 12, 17, 19, 22, 26, 31, 40, 64, 83, 104, 109, 120
Herodotus, 5, 50, 103
Hesiod, 5-6, 13, 26
Hesperides, 6, 39-40
Hestia, 9
Hippomenes, 59, 61
Historic Period, 4
Homer, 1, 4-5, 28, 72, 90, 96, 103, 110, 117
Hyacinthus, 26
Hydra, 34-36
Hylas, 44
Hypsipyle, 99

Ianthe, 145-148
Icarius, 89
Icarus, 77-78
Ida, Mount, 7, 104-105, 109, 112
Iliad, 4, 103, 110
Illyria, 86, 92
Ino, 42, 86-89
Io, 30-32
Iobates, 71
Iocaste, 94, 96
Iolcus (Volos), 2-3, 42, 45
Ionia, 62
Ionian, 4-5, 130, 133
Iphigenia, 106, 114-116
Iris, 7, 9, 22, 75-76, 87
Iron Age, 13

174

smene, 96
Italy, 112-113, 136
Ithaca, 106, 117, 120, 122

Jason, 3, 5, 42, 44-45, 47, 56-57, 99-100
Joppa, 64

Knossos (Cnossus), 2, 4, 16, 54, 77

Labyrinth, 54, 77-78
Laconia, 26, 90
Laertes, 43, 57, 117, 122
Laius, 94, 96
Laocoön, 43, 110
Lamias, 146, 155
Laomedon, 73-74
Lavinium, 113
Leda, 105
Lemnos, 4, 12, 43, 99
Lesbos, 49, 92
Leto, 9, 11, 23-24, 28
Liguria, 130
Linear B Tablets, 2-3
Lotus Eaters, 118
Lycia, 71
Lydia, 20, 62, 133-134

Macedonia, 5, 9
Malea, 4, 36, 118
Marinatos, Prof., 4
Massilia, 130-132
Medea, 44-45, 52, 54, 120
Medusa, 64, 71, 150
Megara, 34, 99, 116
Meleager, 43, 56-58
Melos, 4
Menelaus, 105-106, 116-117
Metis, 7, 11, 62
Midas, 128-129
Minoan, 1-2, 4
Minotaur, 1, 54, 77, 90
Minos, King, 1, 16, 37-38, 54, 77-78, 90
Minyans, 1, 33
Mnemosyne, 11, 26
Monovasia, 3
Moros, 11
Mycenae, 1-2, 106, 114-116
Mycenaean, 1-5, 43, 50, 96, 116
Myrmidons, 104, 106, 108
Muses, 9, 11, 26, 28

Nannos, 130-131
Narcissus, 79-80
Nauplia, 2
Nausicaa, 122
Naxos, 12, 54, 90
Nemean Games, 43, 98-100

Neoptolemus, 4, 110, 117
Nereid, 104, 110, 142, 145, 147-150, 156, 158, 167-168
Nereus, 6
Nessus (Centaur), 34, 41
Nilssen, Dr., 100
Nestor, King, 3, 57, 106, 117
Niobe, 27-29

Oceanus, 6-7, 125
Odysseus, 4, 12, 43, 63, 96, 103, 106, 108, 117-122
Odyssey, 5, 103, 117, 122
Oedipus, 94-97
Olympiad, 1
Olympus, Mount, 5, 7-9, 12, 14-15, 17, 21-22, 25-26, 30-31, 41, 62-63, 70, 72, 87
Orchomenus, 1, 33
Orestes, 114-116
Orpheus, 43, 47-49
Ossa, Mount, 8, 25
Othrys, Mount, 7

Pelasgiotis, 65
Pan, 19, 31, 128-129
Pandion, 123
Pandora, 12-15
Parnassus, Mount, 15, 24-26
Paris, 103-105, 107, 110, 117
Patroclus, 106-108, 110
Pegasus, 63, 71-72, 150
Peleus, 3, 43, 47, 57, 64, 104
Pelion, Mount, 8, 25, 36, 47, 104
Peloponnese, 1, 4, 35, 37, 48, 52, 106
Pelops, 94
Pentheus, 86, 90, 92
Persephone, 20-22, 48, 68-69
Perdix, 77
Perseus, 19, 63-65
Persians, 50, 65, 134-135, 137
Phaethon, 125-127
Phaistos, 4
Philomela, 123-124
Philomen, 83-84
Phrixus, 42, 87
Phrygia, 89-90, 134
Pliny, 127
Pollux, 33, 57, 105
Polycrates, 136-138
Polyneices, 96-98
Pompey, 132
Poseidon, 2, 5, 9, 11, 23, 37-38, 45, 50-51, 65, 73, 77, 115, 120, 122, 150
Potnia, 2
Priam, King, 25, 105, 107, 109-110, 112
Procne, 123-124
Prometheus, 12, 14-15, 36, 40, 63

175

Prosymna, 2
Proëtus, 64, 71
Protis, 130-131
Psyche, 66-70
Pygmalion, 81-82
Pylades, 114-115
Pylus, 1-3, 106, 117
Pythagorus, 136
Python, 24

Rhea, 6-7, 20, 22
Rhodes, 4
Rhodus *Argonautica*, 45

Samos, 136-137
Santorini (Thera), 4
Sardis, 133-135, 137
Schliemann, Heinrich, 1, 103
Scylla and Charybdis, 45, 121
Selene, 9, 12, 126
Semele, 86-87, 89, 92
Sicily, 8, 12, 20, 39, 45, 78, 112, 121
Sinon, 110
Sirens, 121
Skyros, 4, 55
Solon, 133, 135
Somnus, 76
Sophocles, 5, 96, 103
Sunion, 54, 77
Spain, 130
Sparta, 1-2, 103, 105, 116, 136-137
Sparti, 85-86, 90-91, 94, 99.
Sphinx, 95-96
Stables of Augeias, 37
Symplegades, 44, 47
Syria, 4, 90

Tantalus, 87, 94, 114
Tartarus, 6-7, 12
Taygetus, Mount, 3
Tempe, Vale of, 25

Teresias, 86
Theban 3, 97-98, 120
Thebes, 1, 3, 27-29, 33, 85-86, 92, 94-99, 101, 107, 123
Themis, 9, 11, 15
Theogony, 5
Thrace, 26, 47, 85, 89-90, 123
Theseus, 1, 4, 52, 54-55, 57, 71, 78, 90, 105
Thessaly, 2, 5, 9, 25, 42, 65, 89, 104
Thessalians, 107
Thetis, 4, 6, 104, 108-110, 117
Thrace, 26, 90, 123
Thrice-Noble, 154-159
Tiphys, 43-44
Tiryns, 1-2, 33-35, 41
Titans, 6-8, 14, 118
Tritons, 11, 165
Trojan Horse, 110
Trojan War, 1, 3-5, 43, 98, 103-104, 114, 117
Trojans, 5, 73, 107-110, 112
Troy, 1, 13, 25, 72-73, 103, 105-107, 109-112, 114, 117, 120
Turkish, 136, 142
Turks, 5, 169
Typhon, 8, 19, 40

Underworld, 11, 19-22, 40-41, 48, 68, 87, 92, 101, 110, 120
Uranus, 6-8, 11-12, 48

Virgil, 113
Volos (Iolcus), 2-3, 42, 45

Wild Man, 139-140, 142-144

Zepherus, 26, 66-67
Zeus, 2, 7-9, 11-17, 19-20, 22-24, 26-28, 30-31, 33, 39, 41-42, 51, 62, 64, 68, 70, 73, 79, 83-84, 87, 89, 98, 102, 104-105, 109, 118, 122, 127